MY FAVORITE FLOWERS

COLORING BOOK

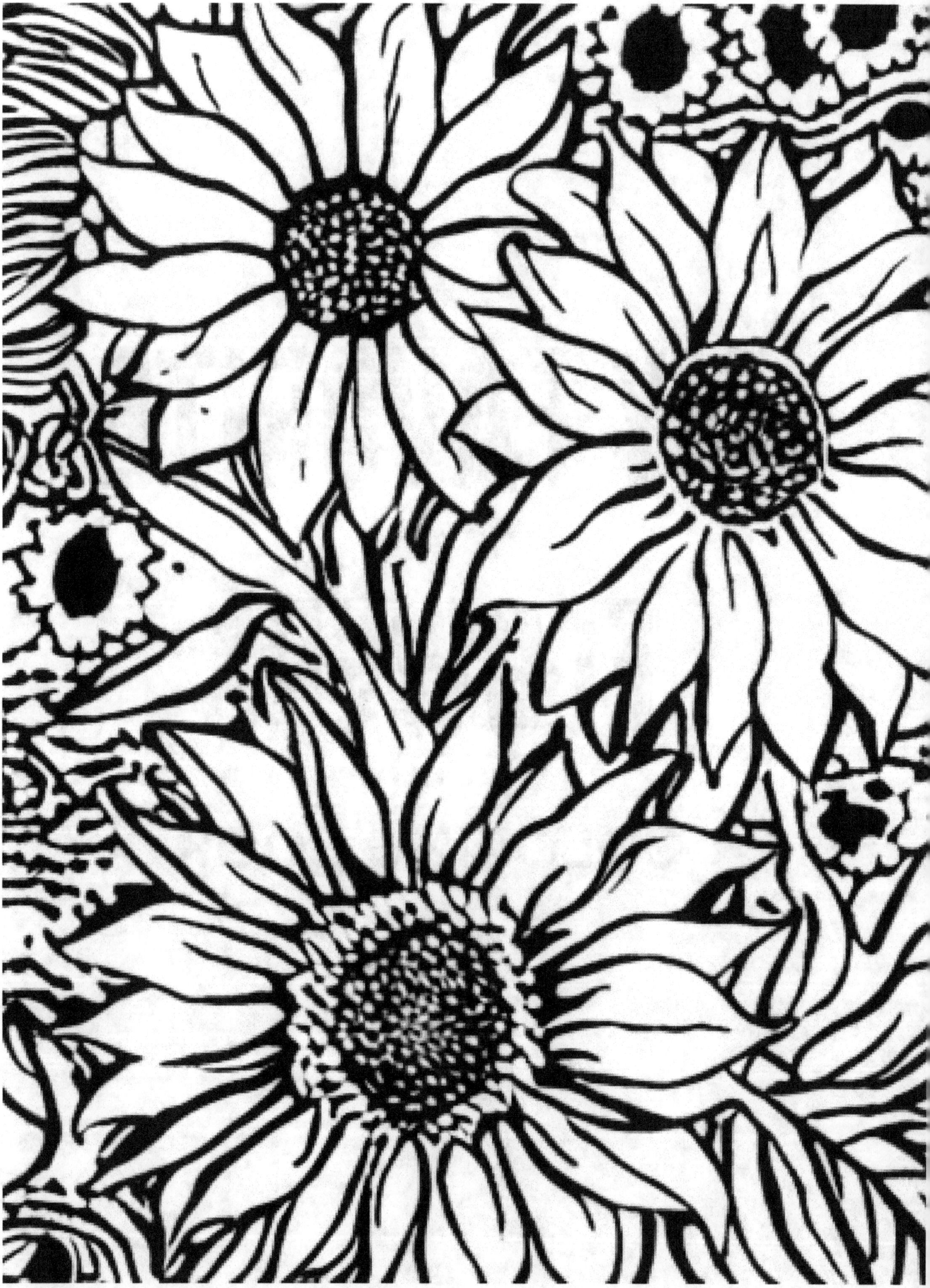

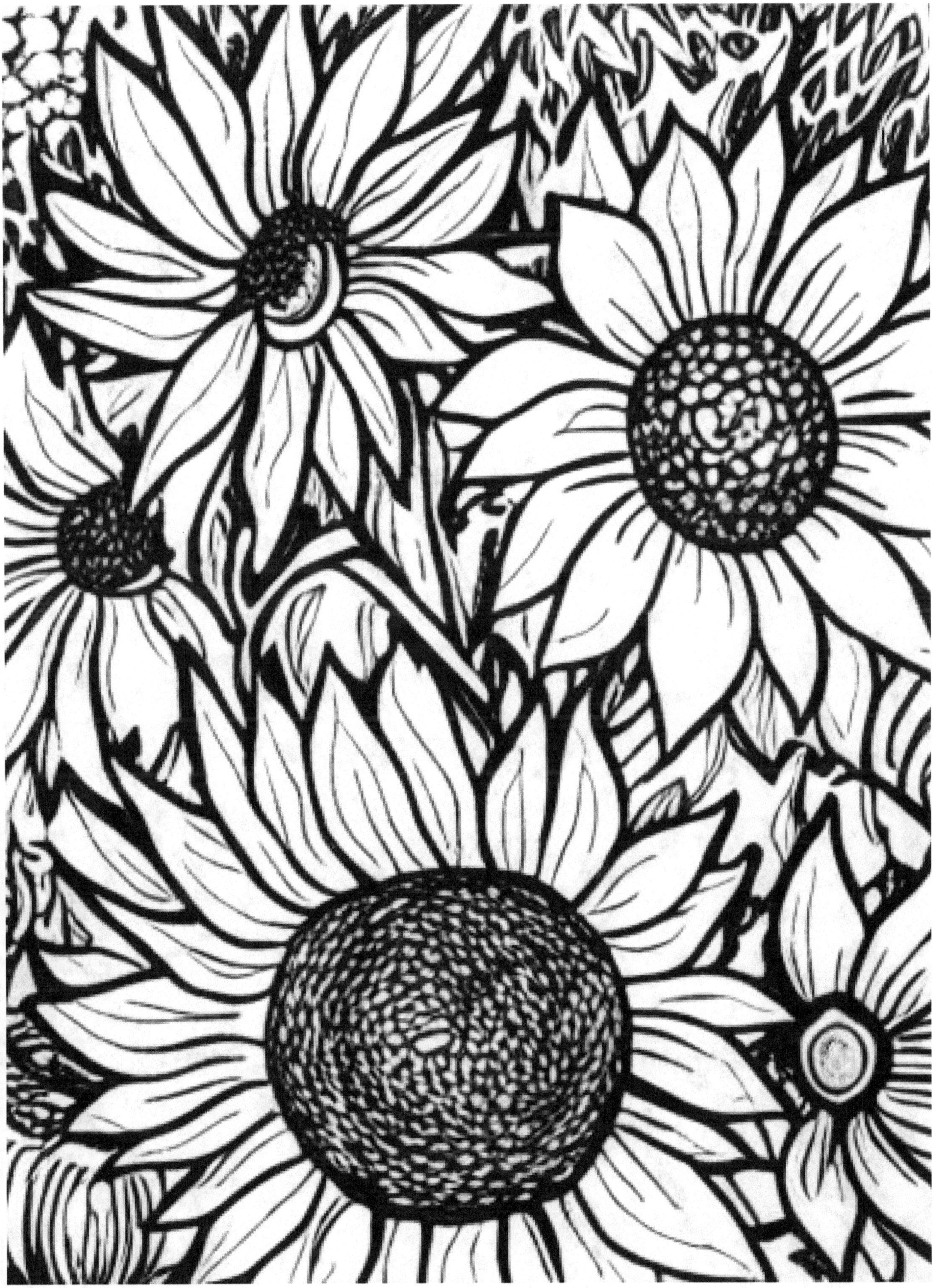

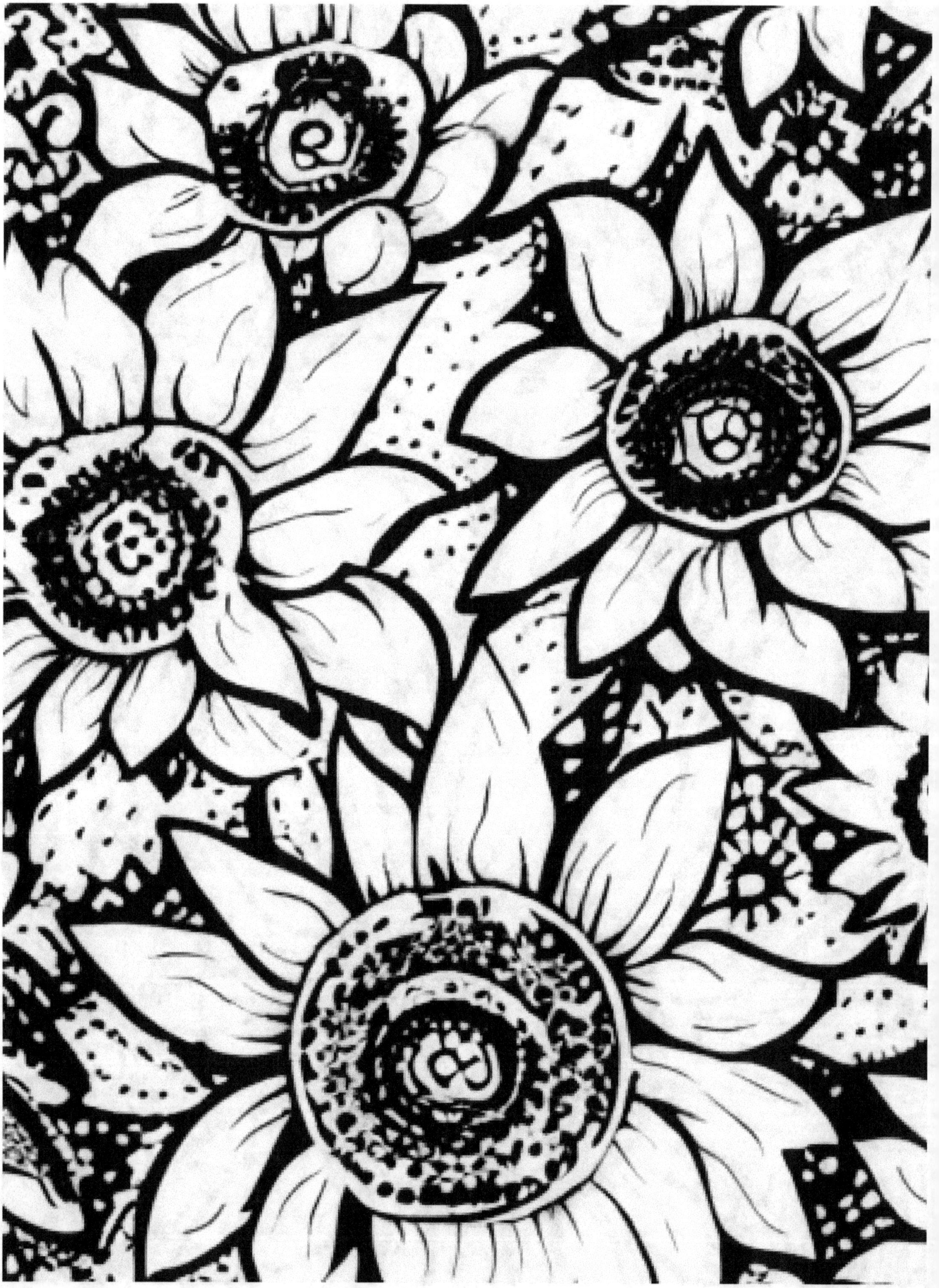

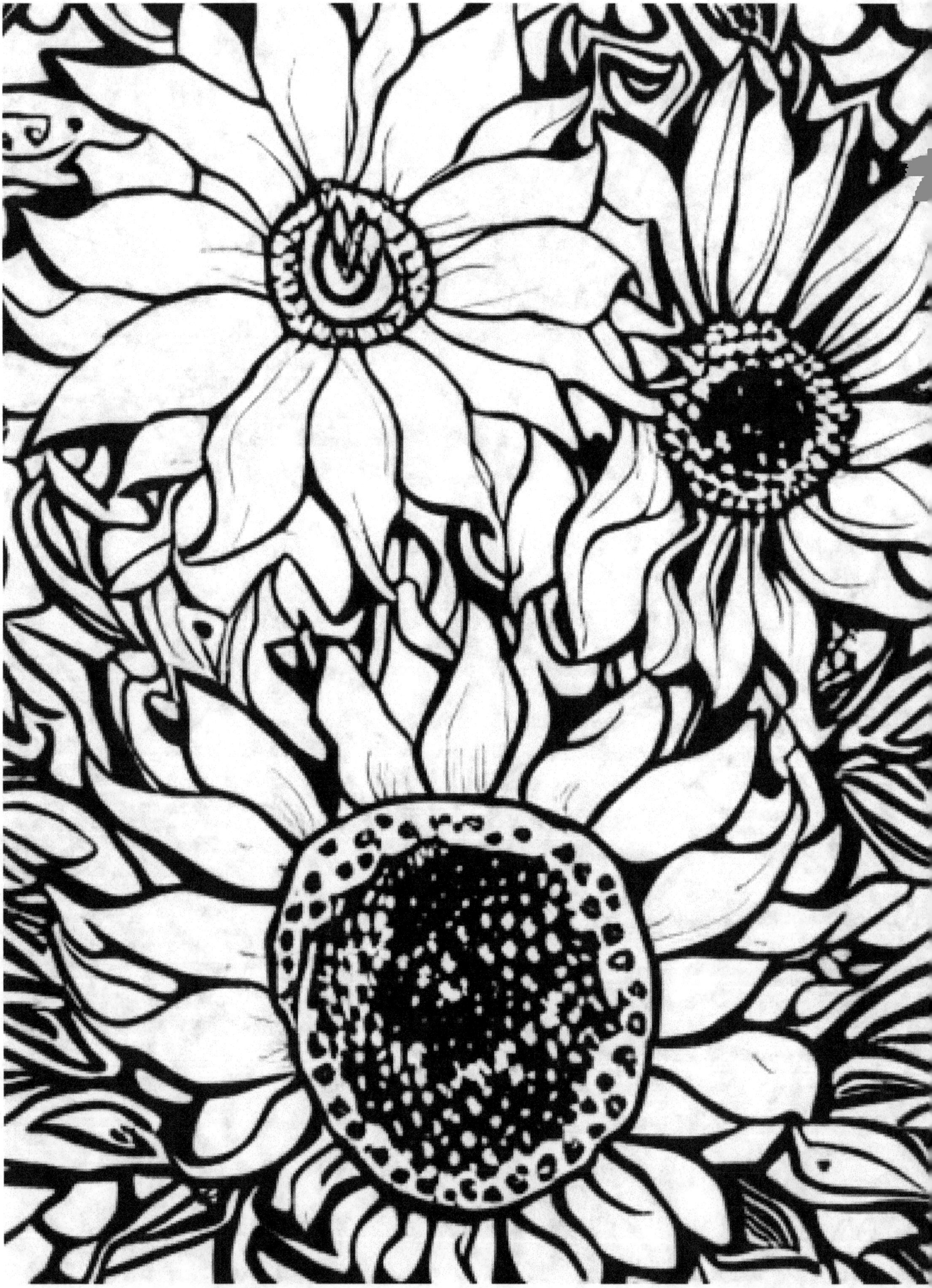

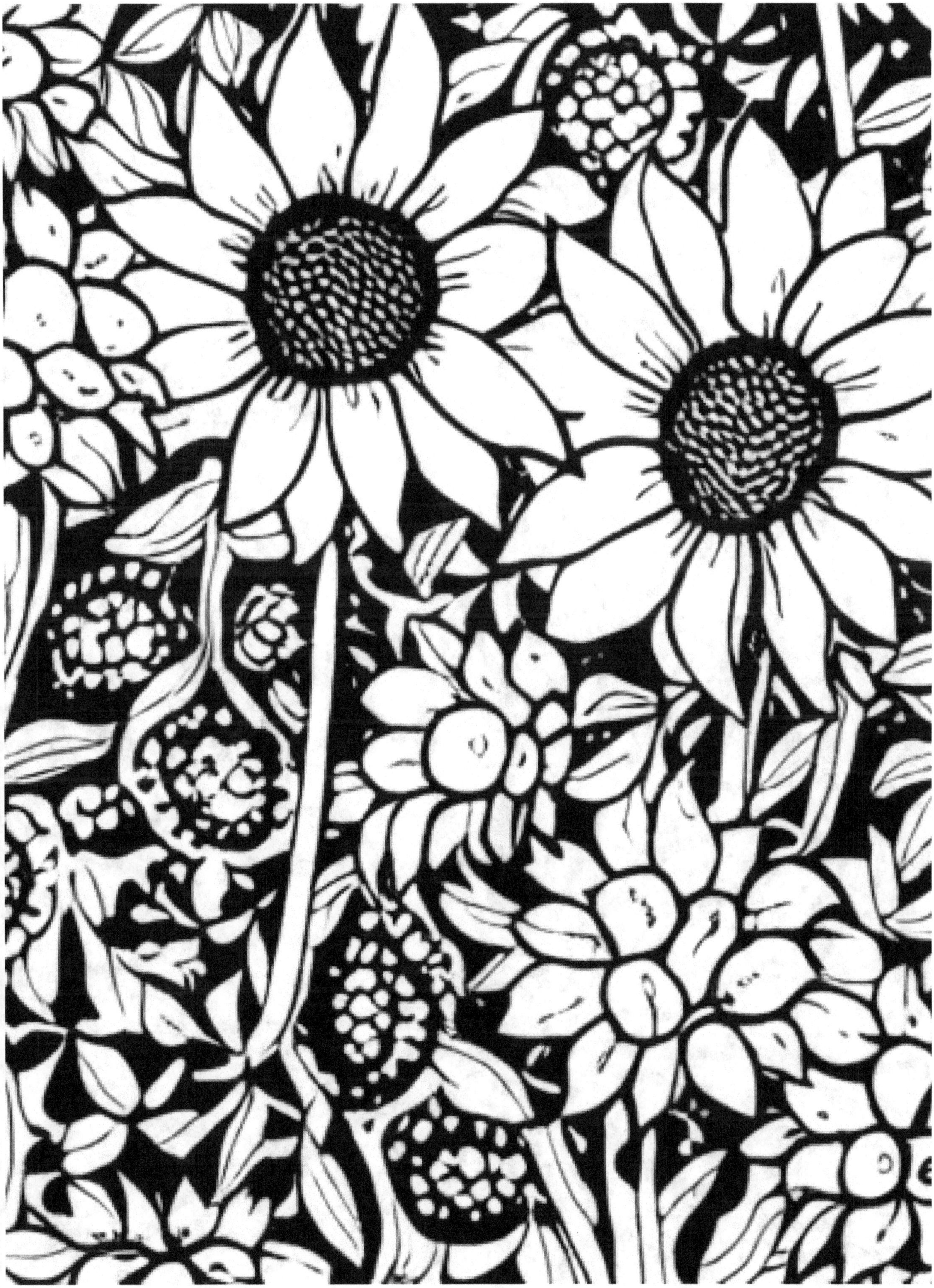

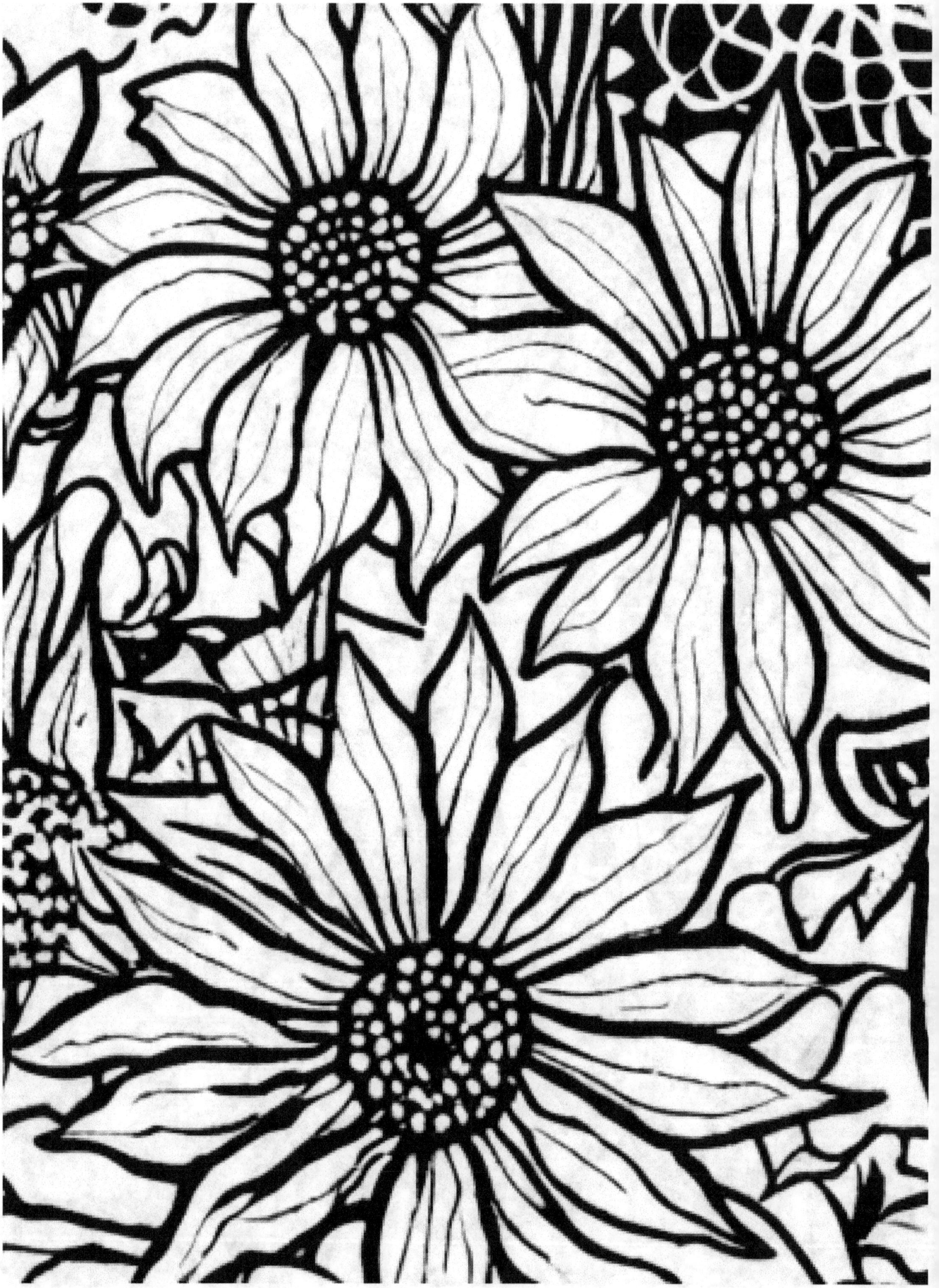

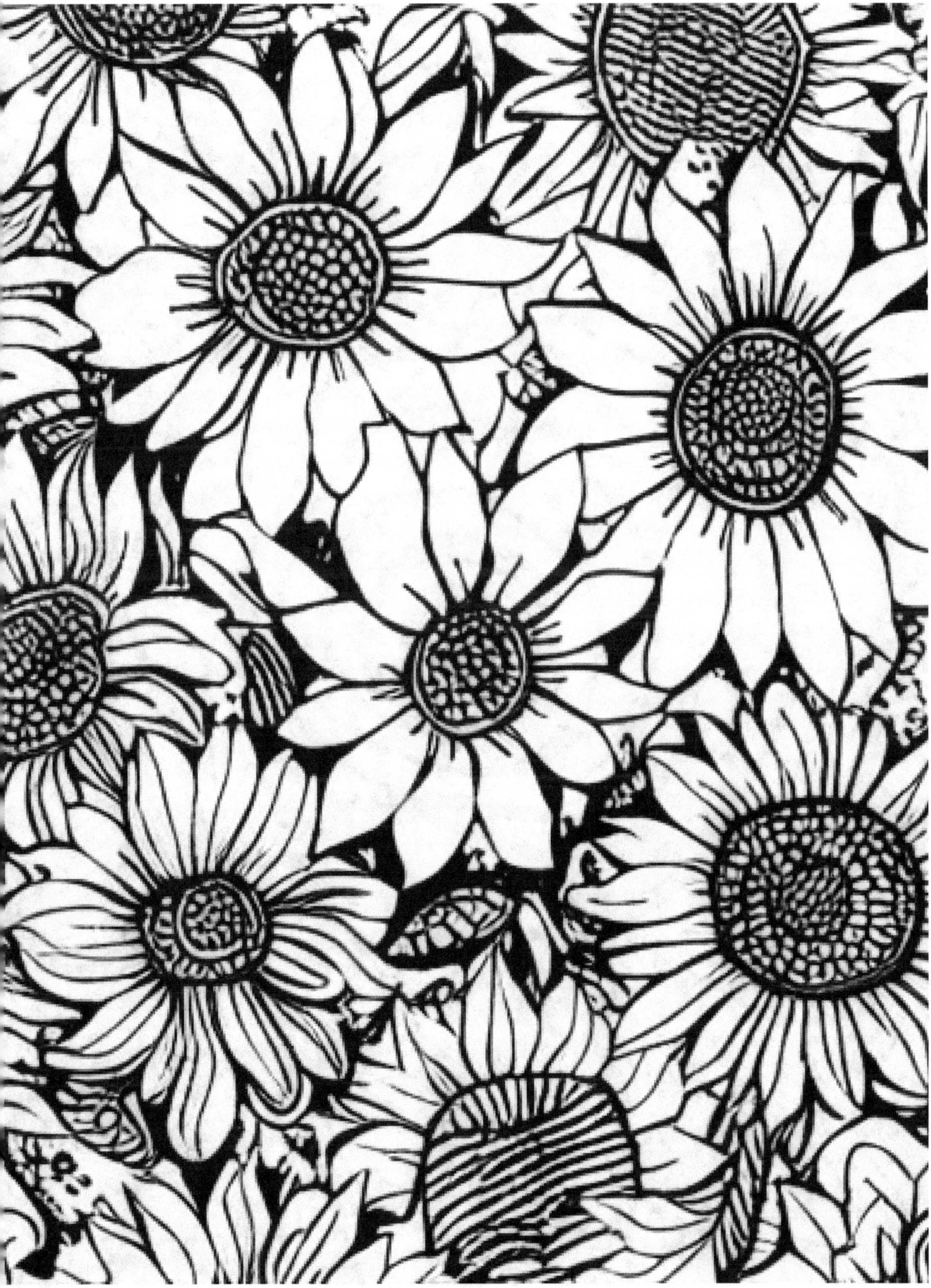

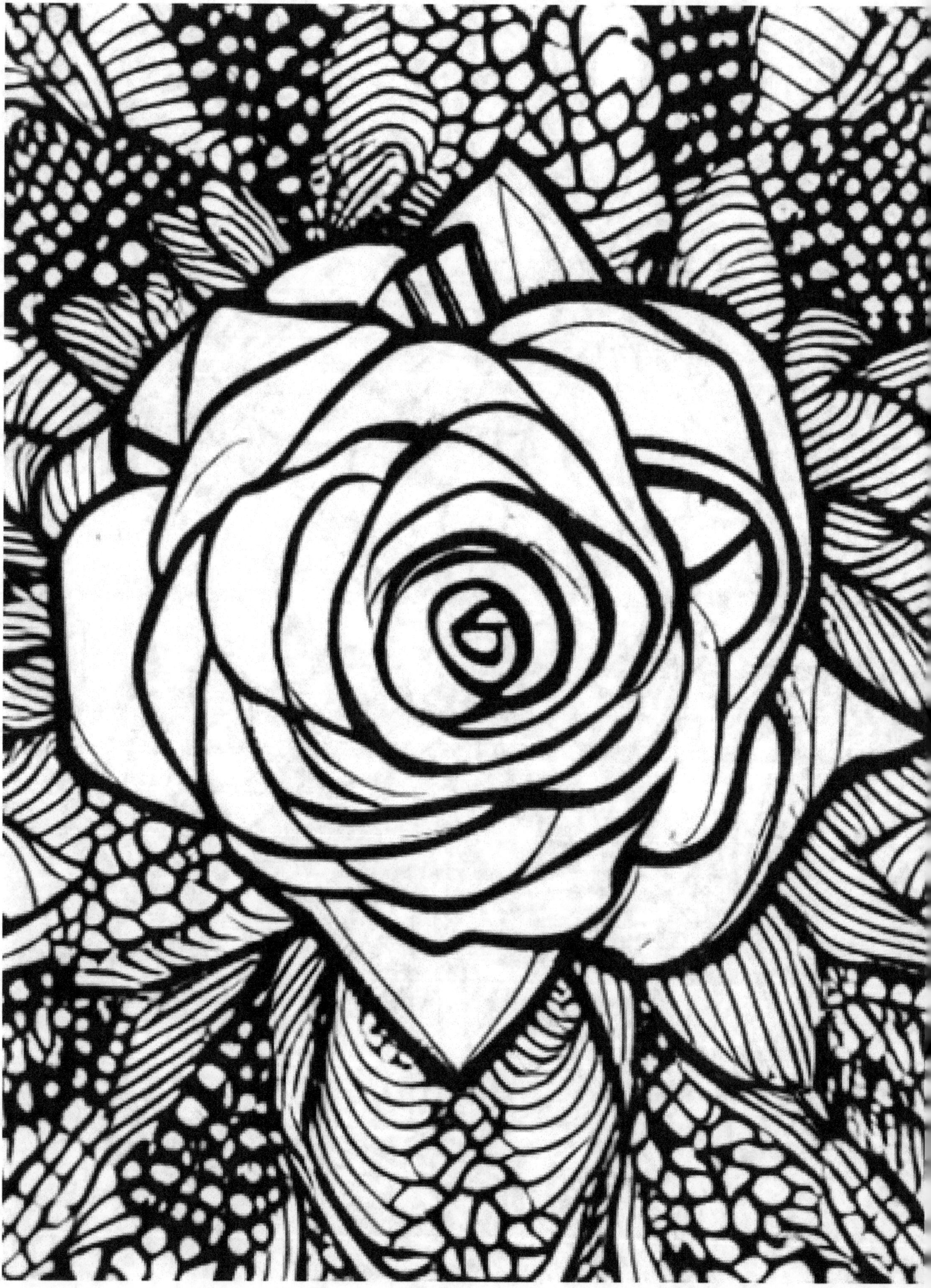

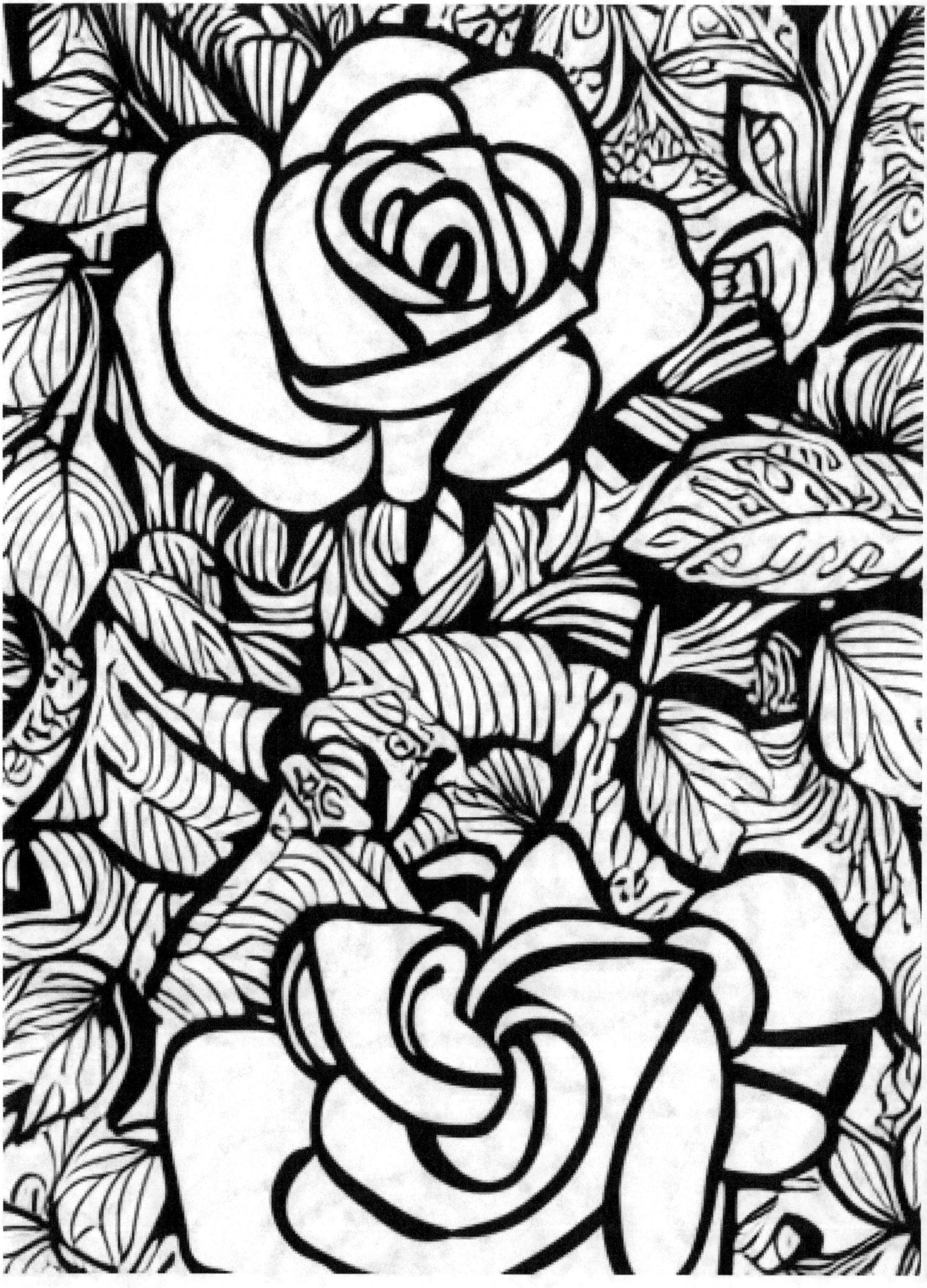

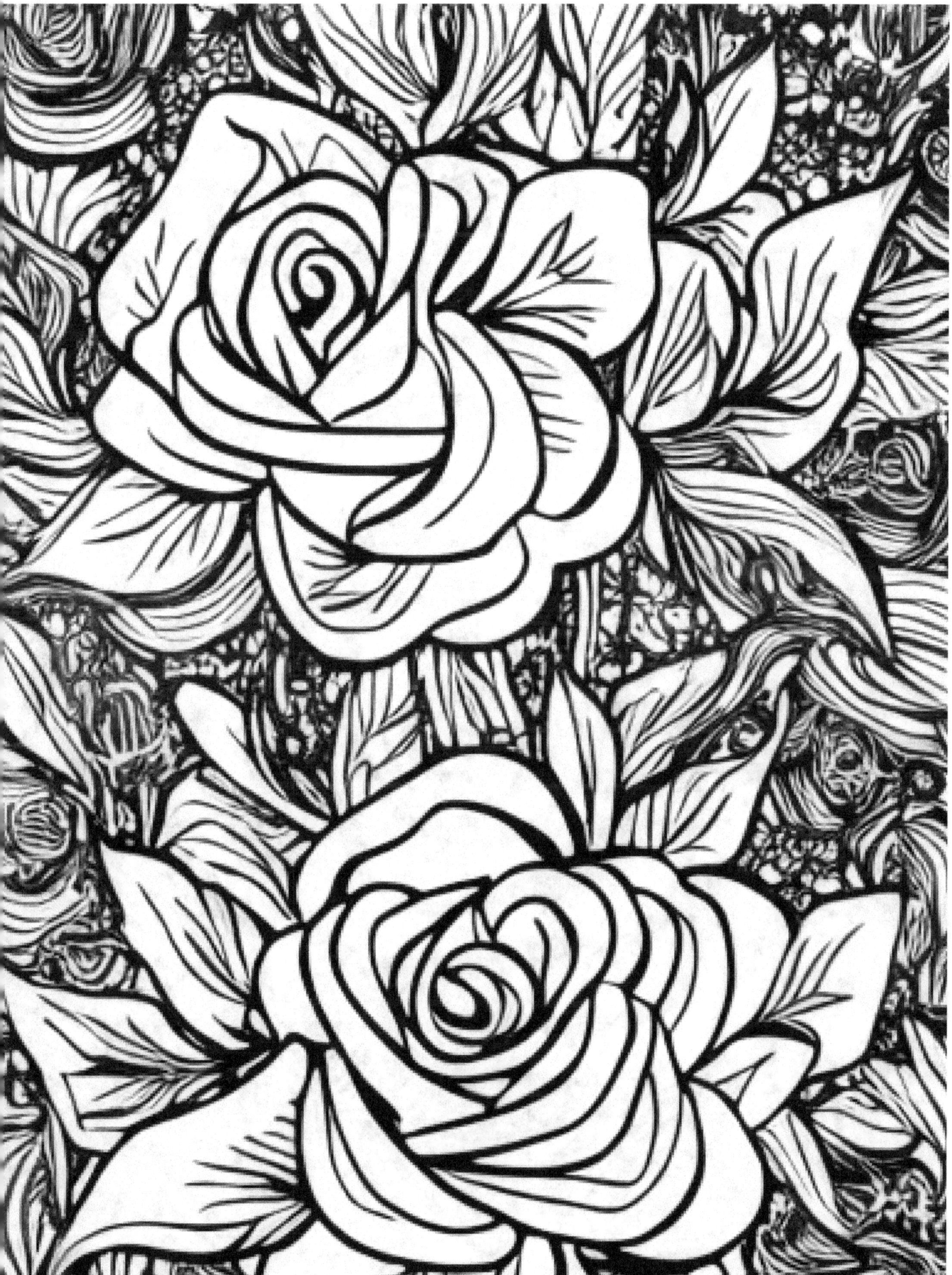

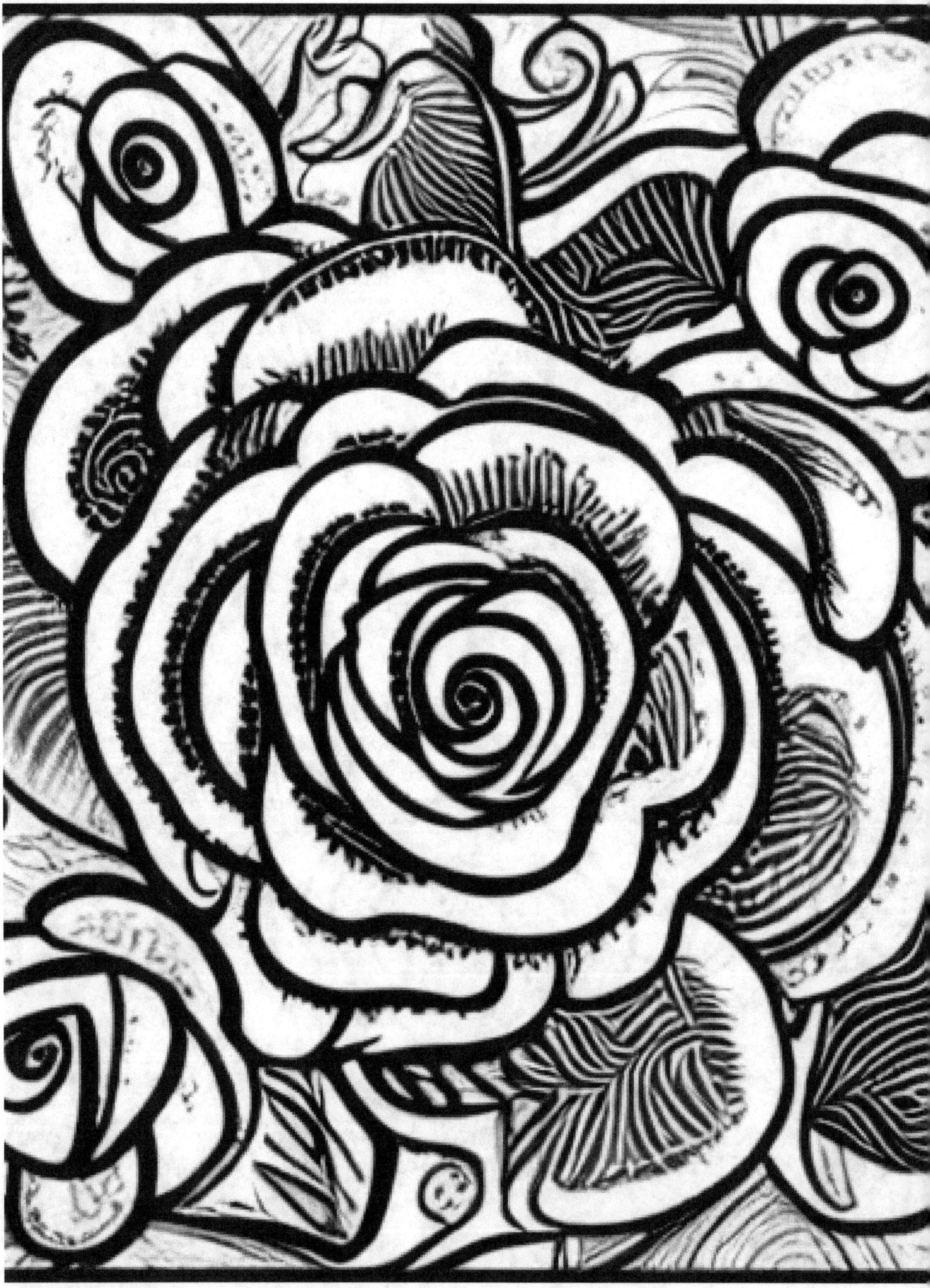

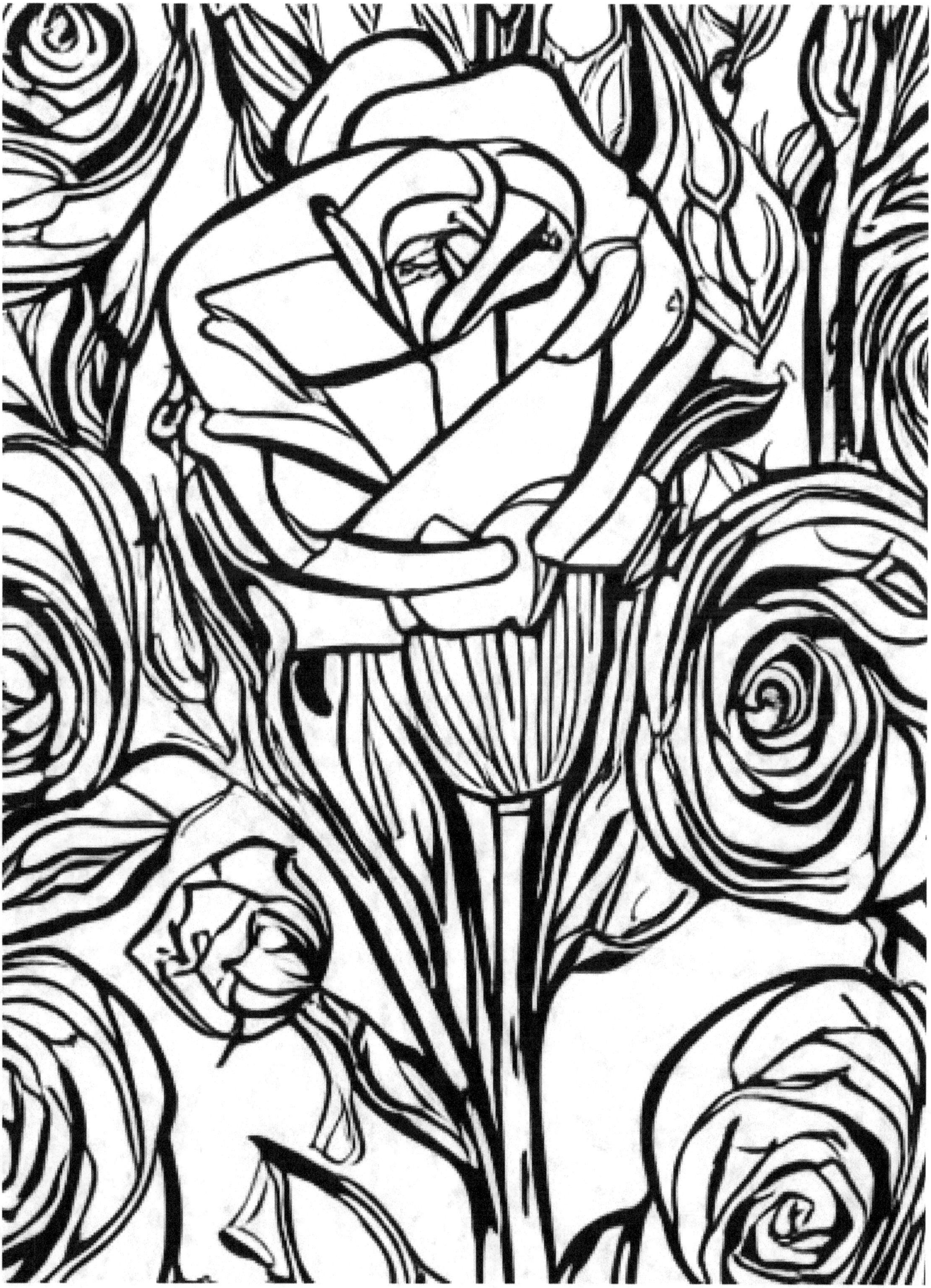

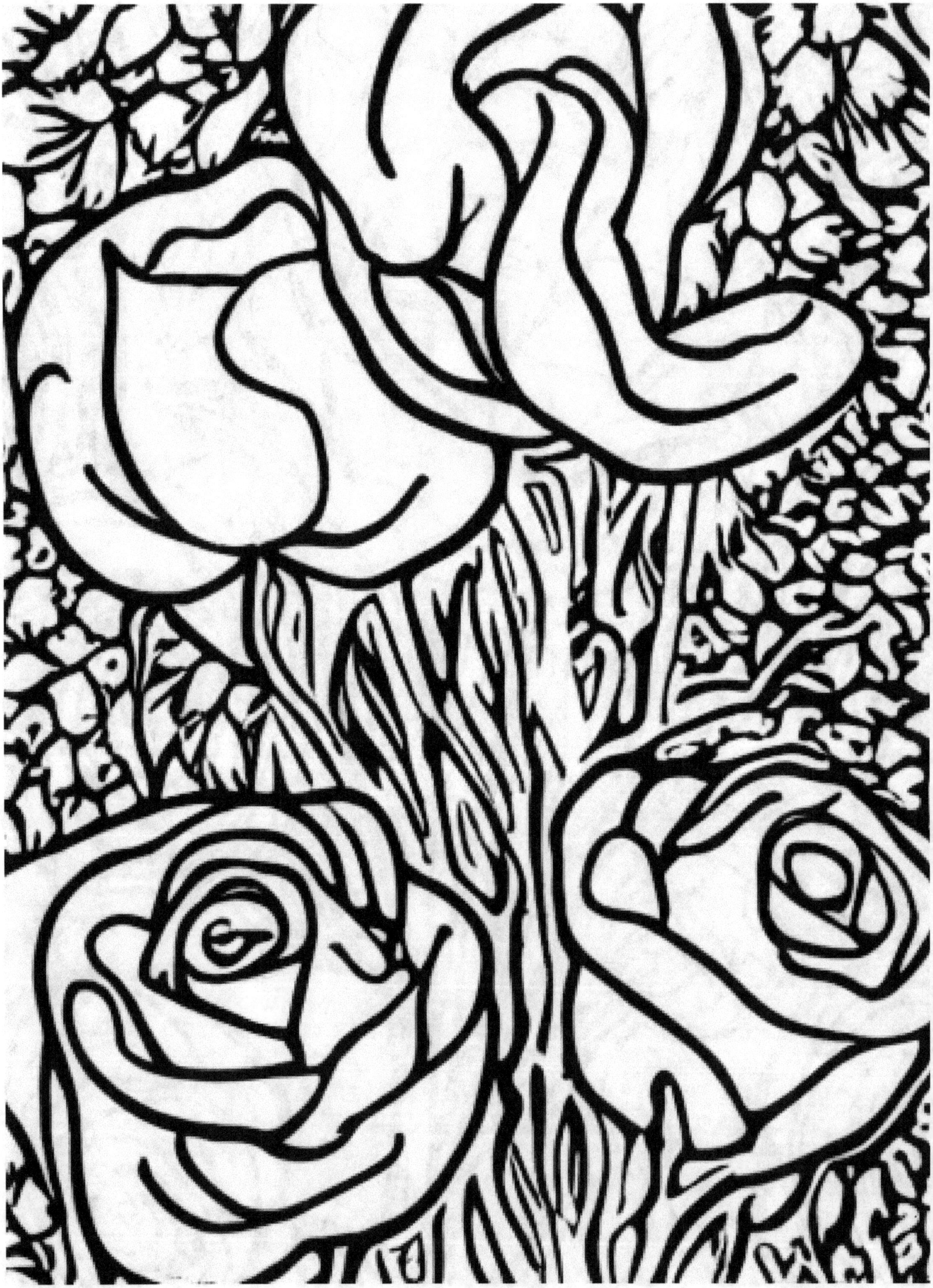

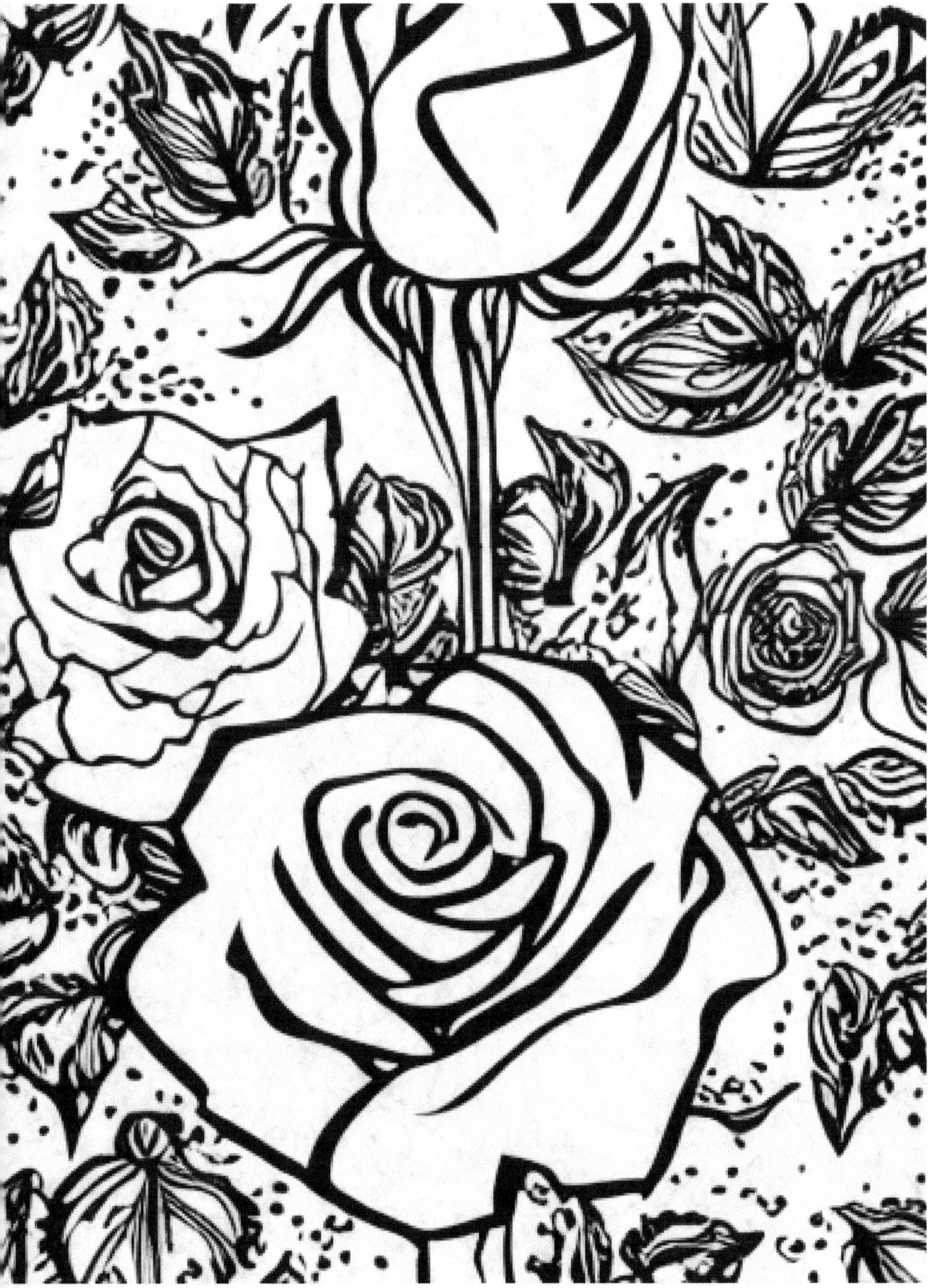

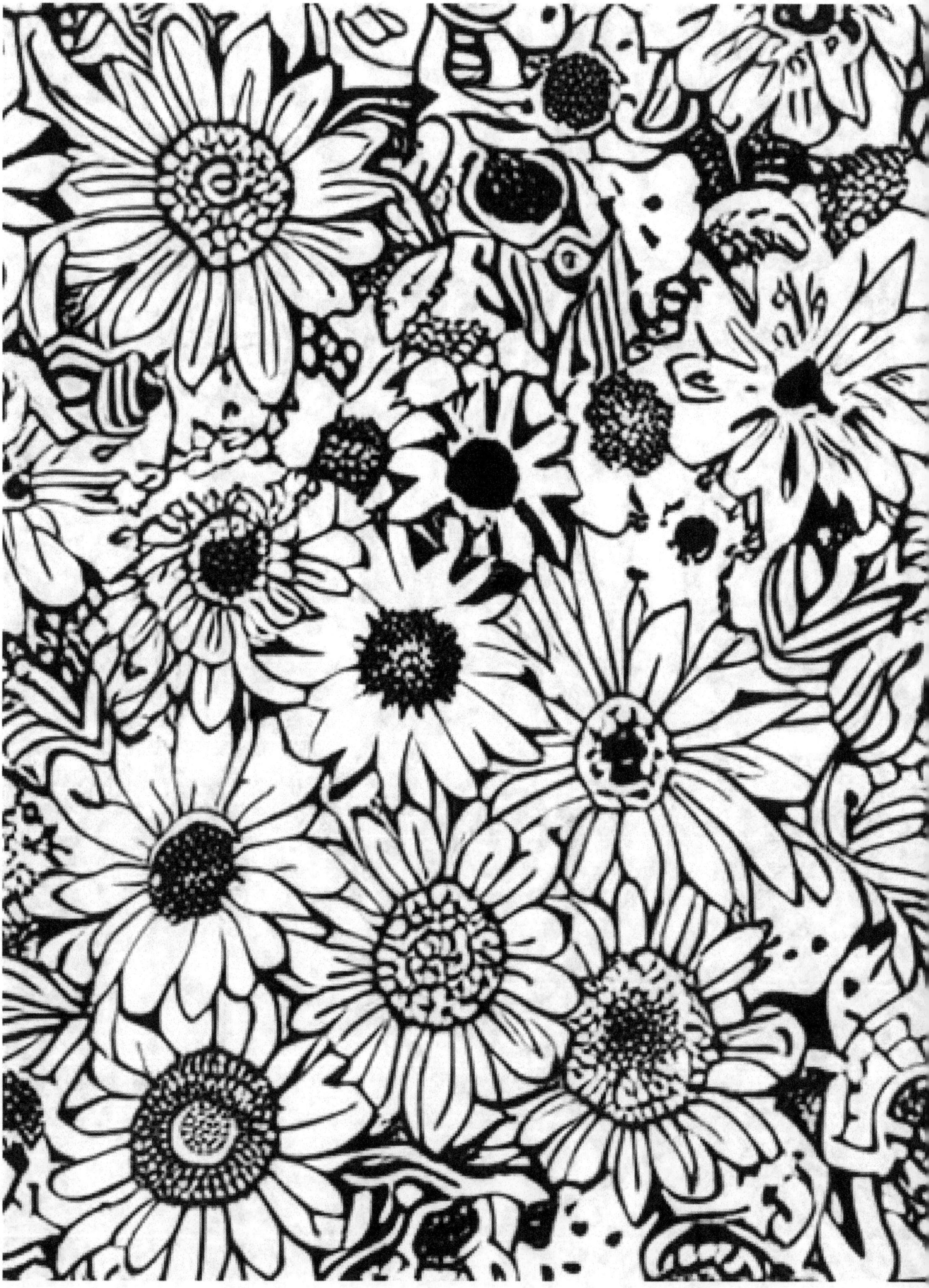

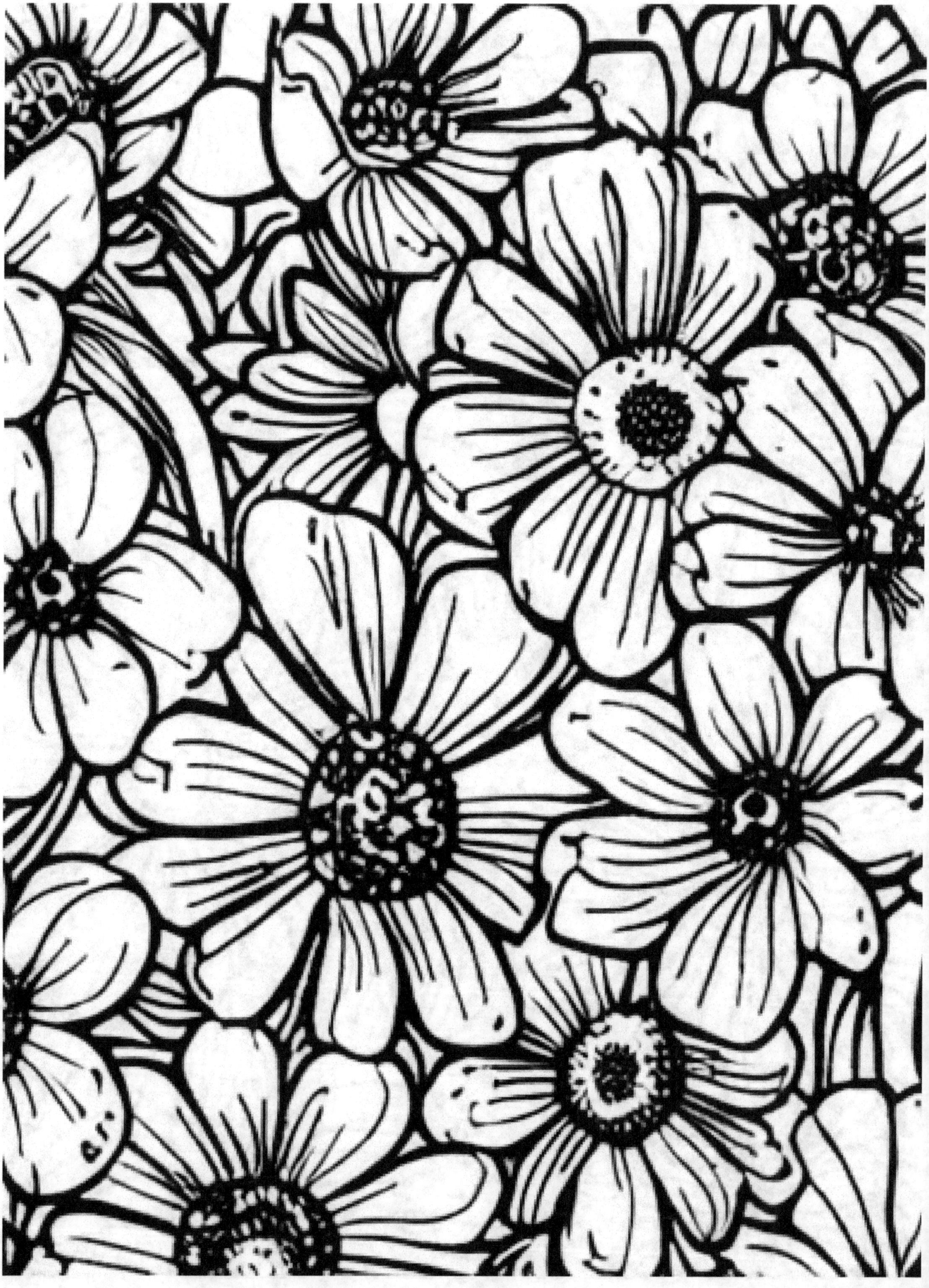

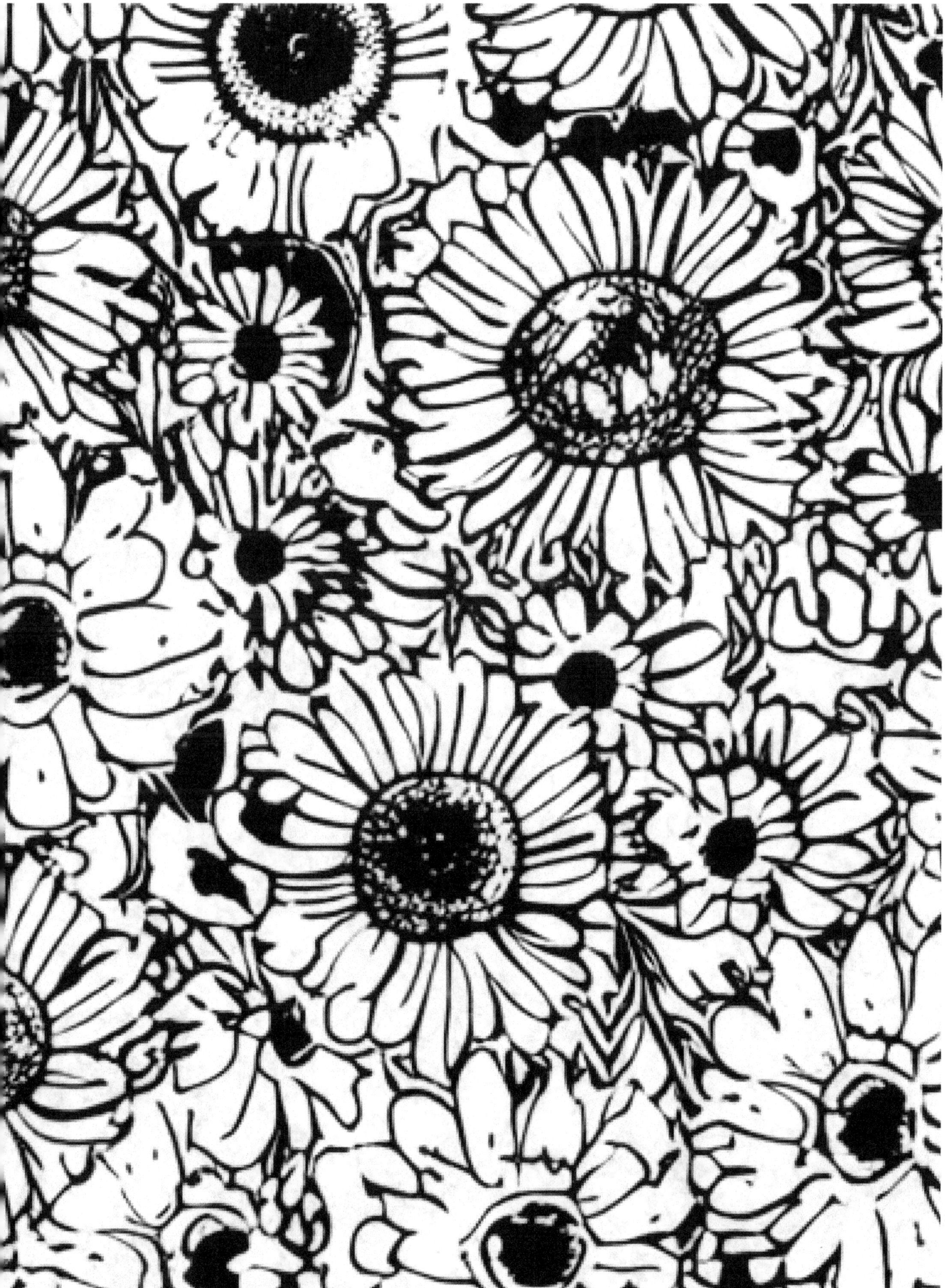

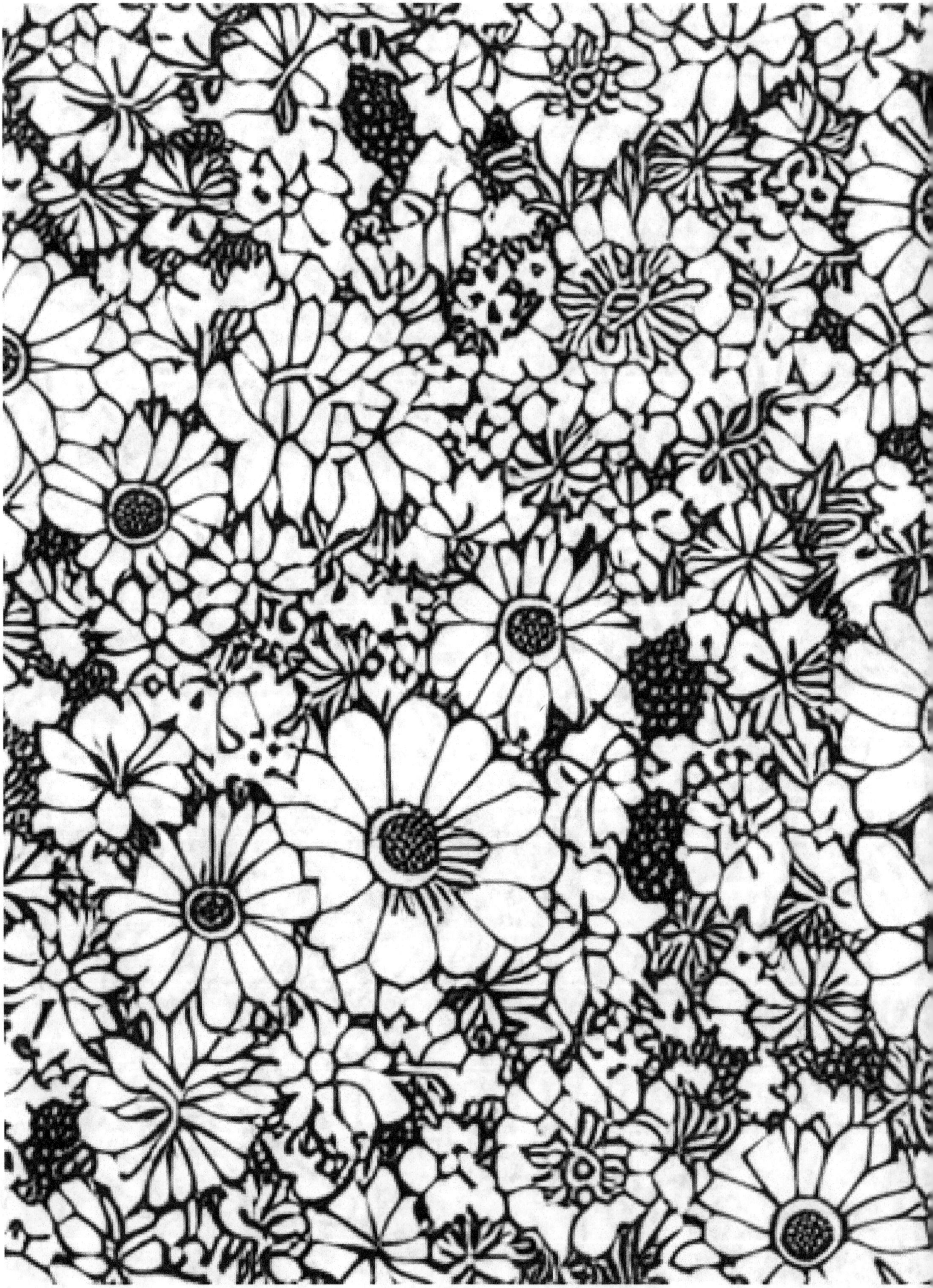

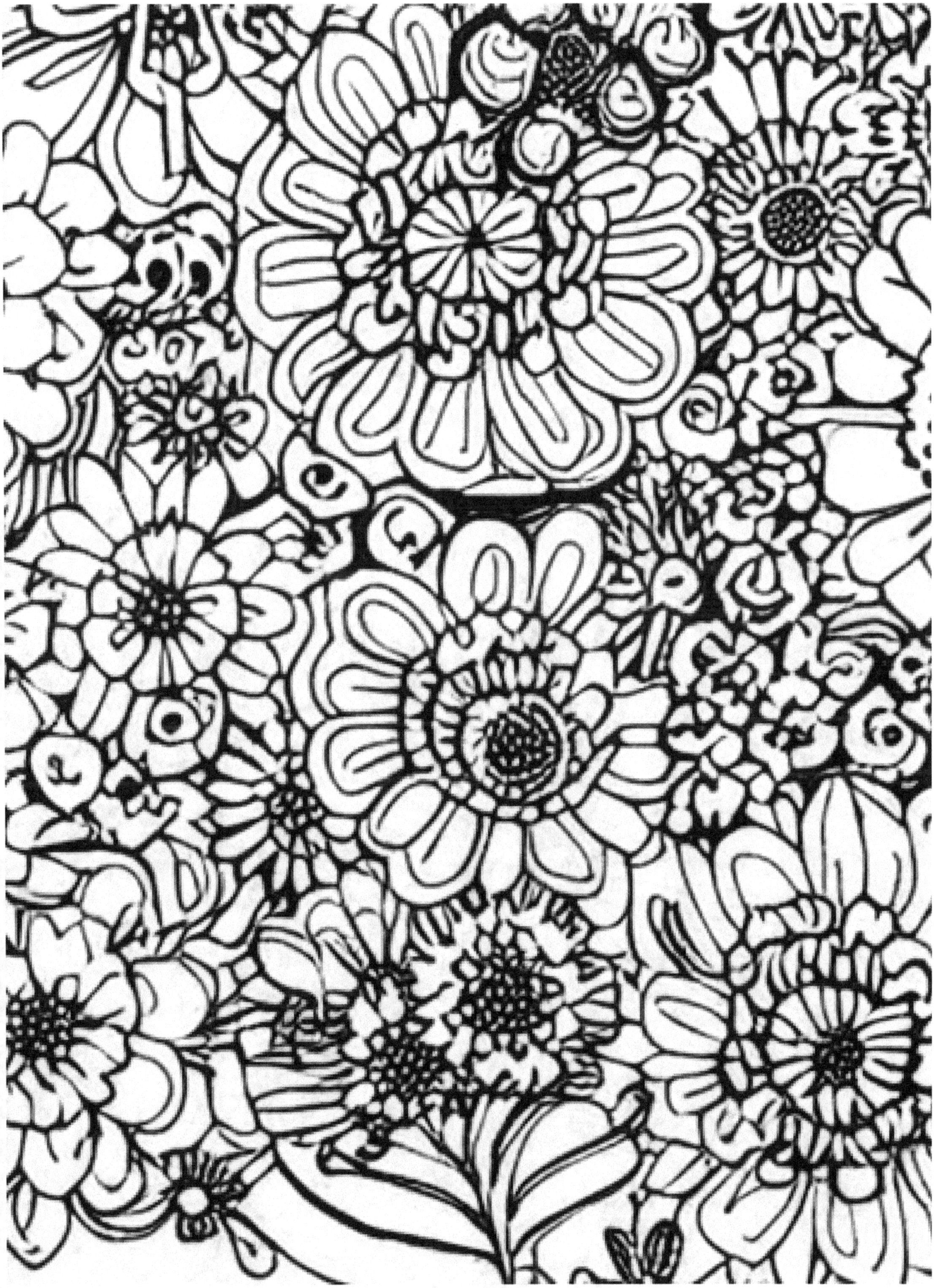

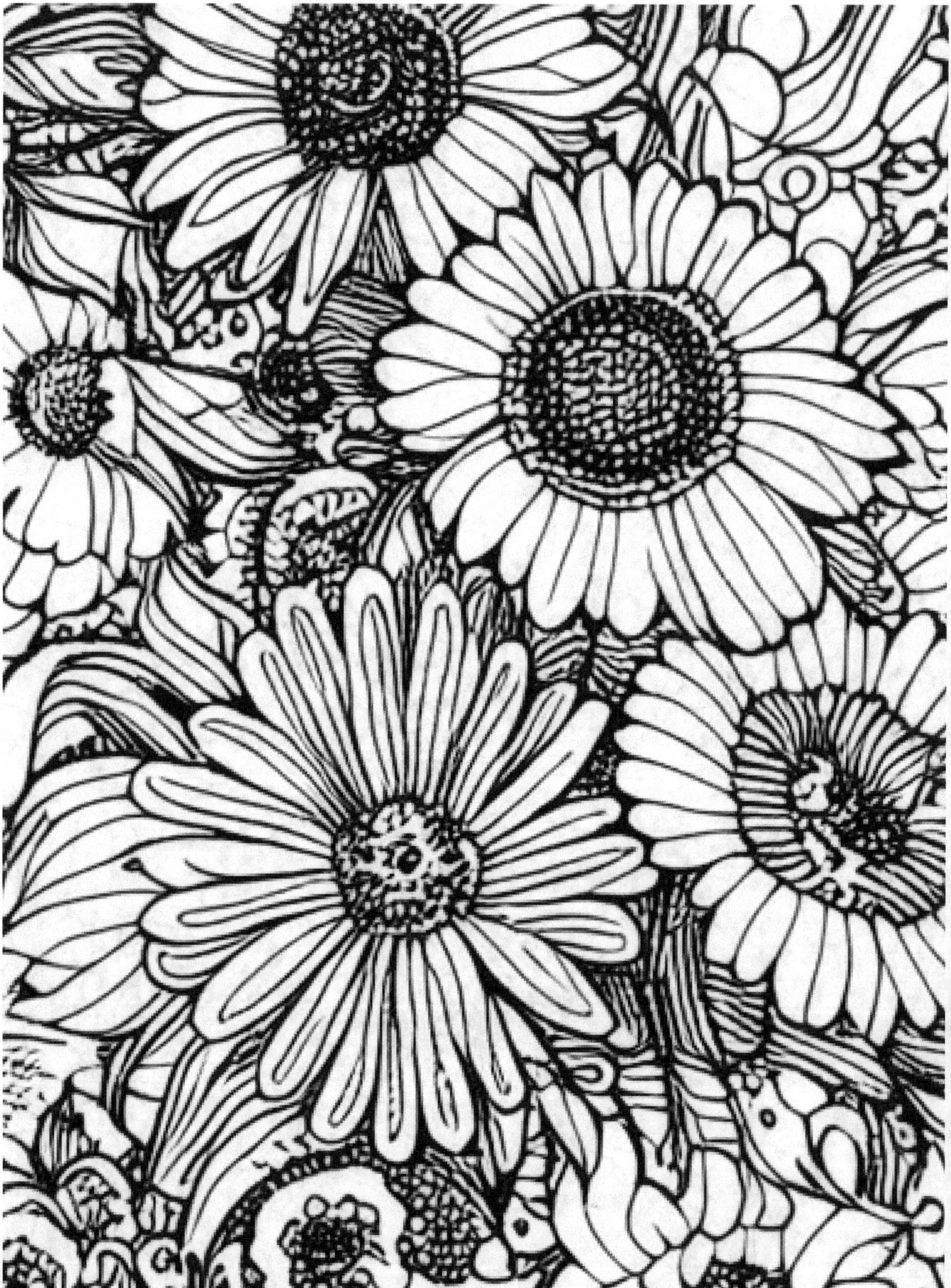

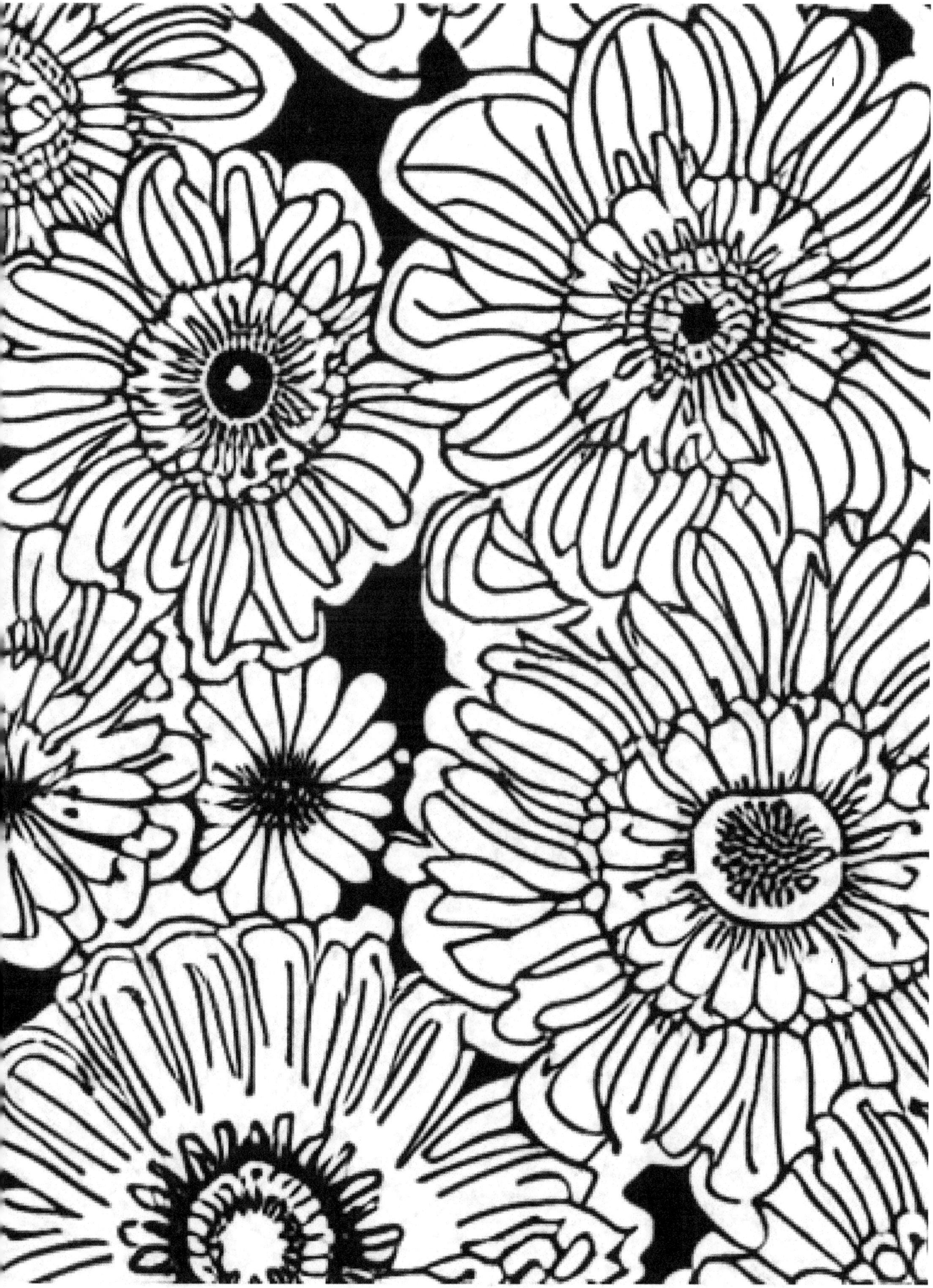

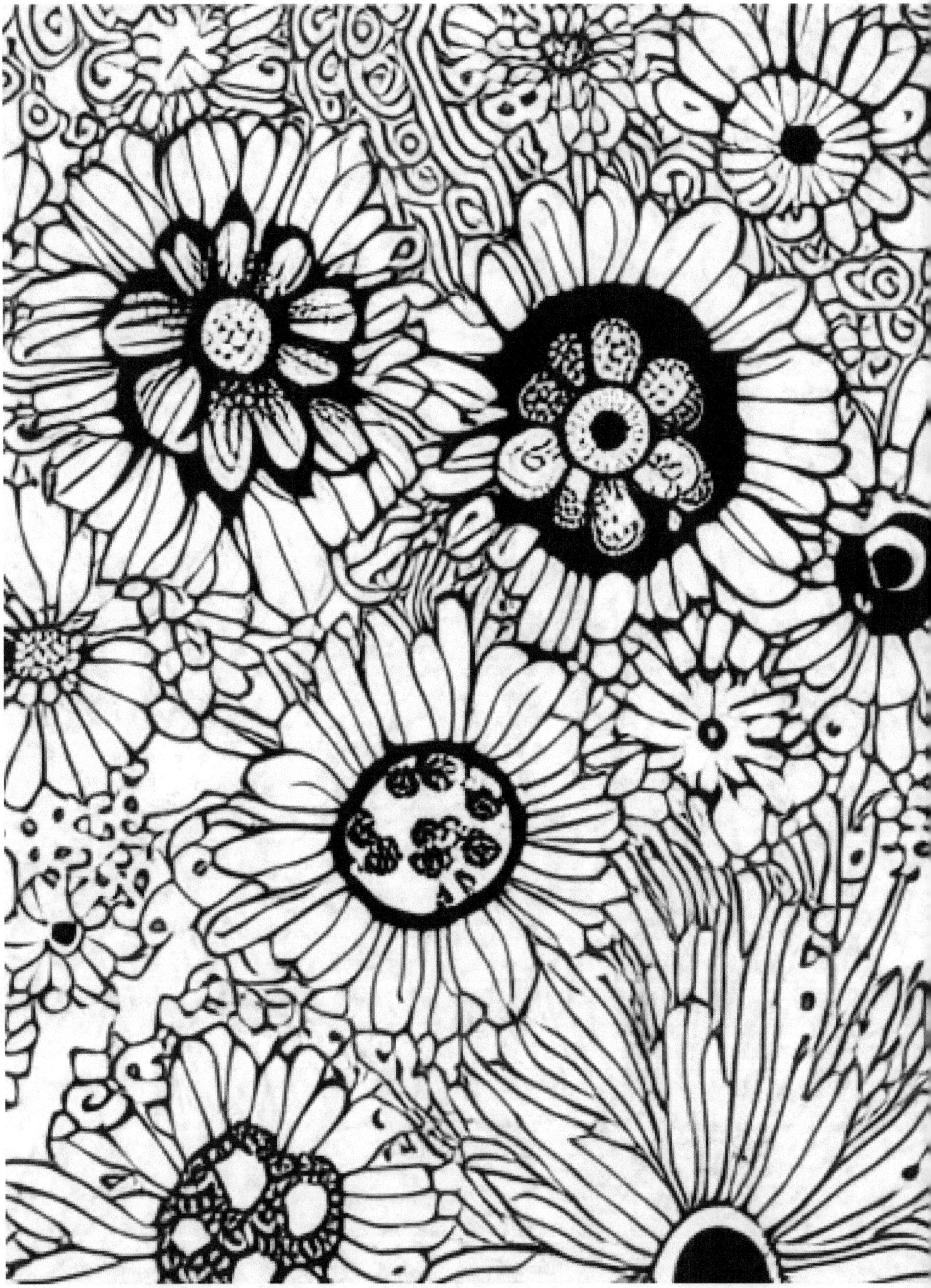

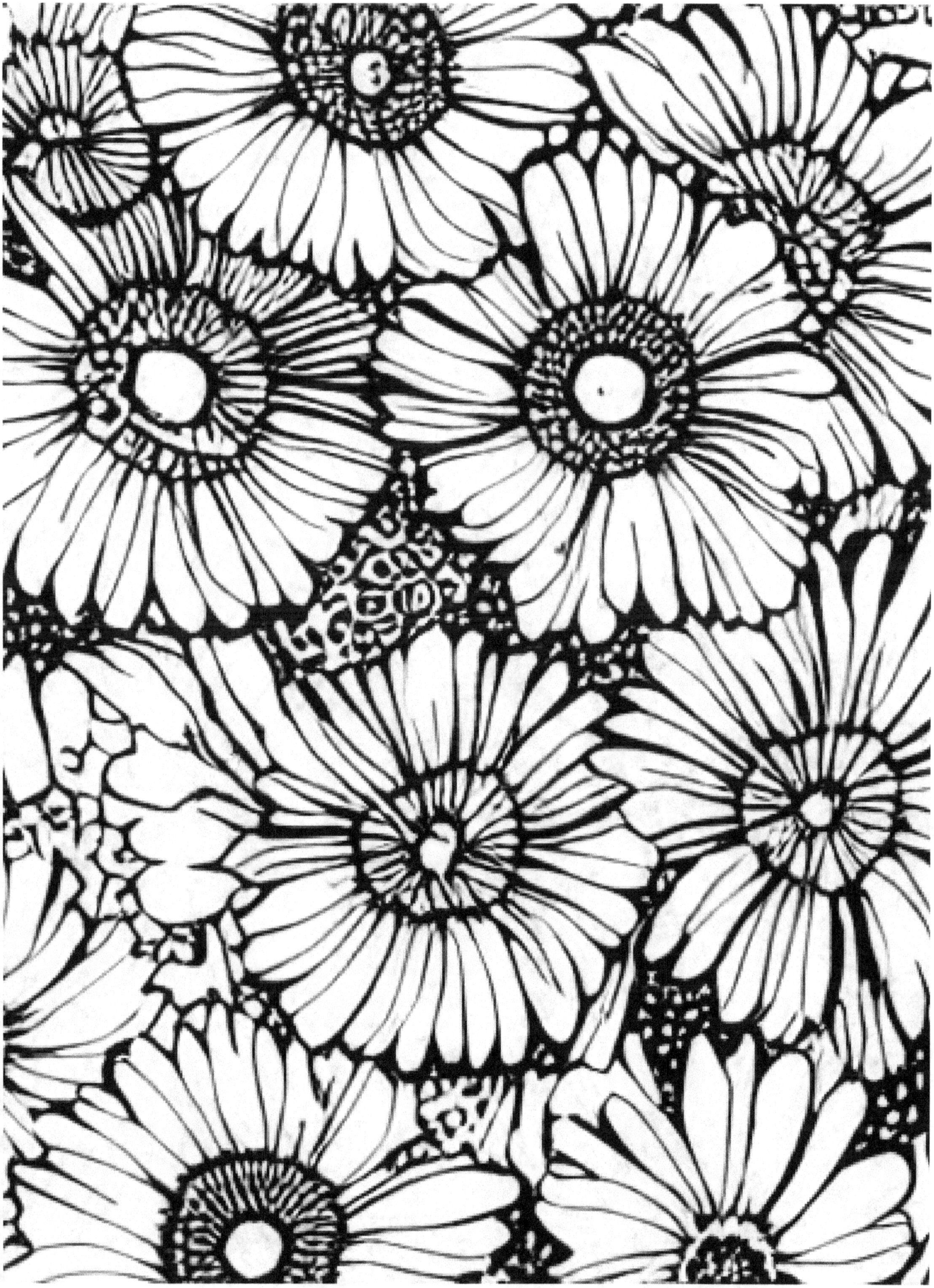

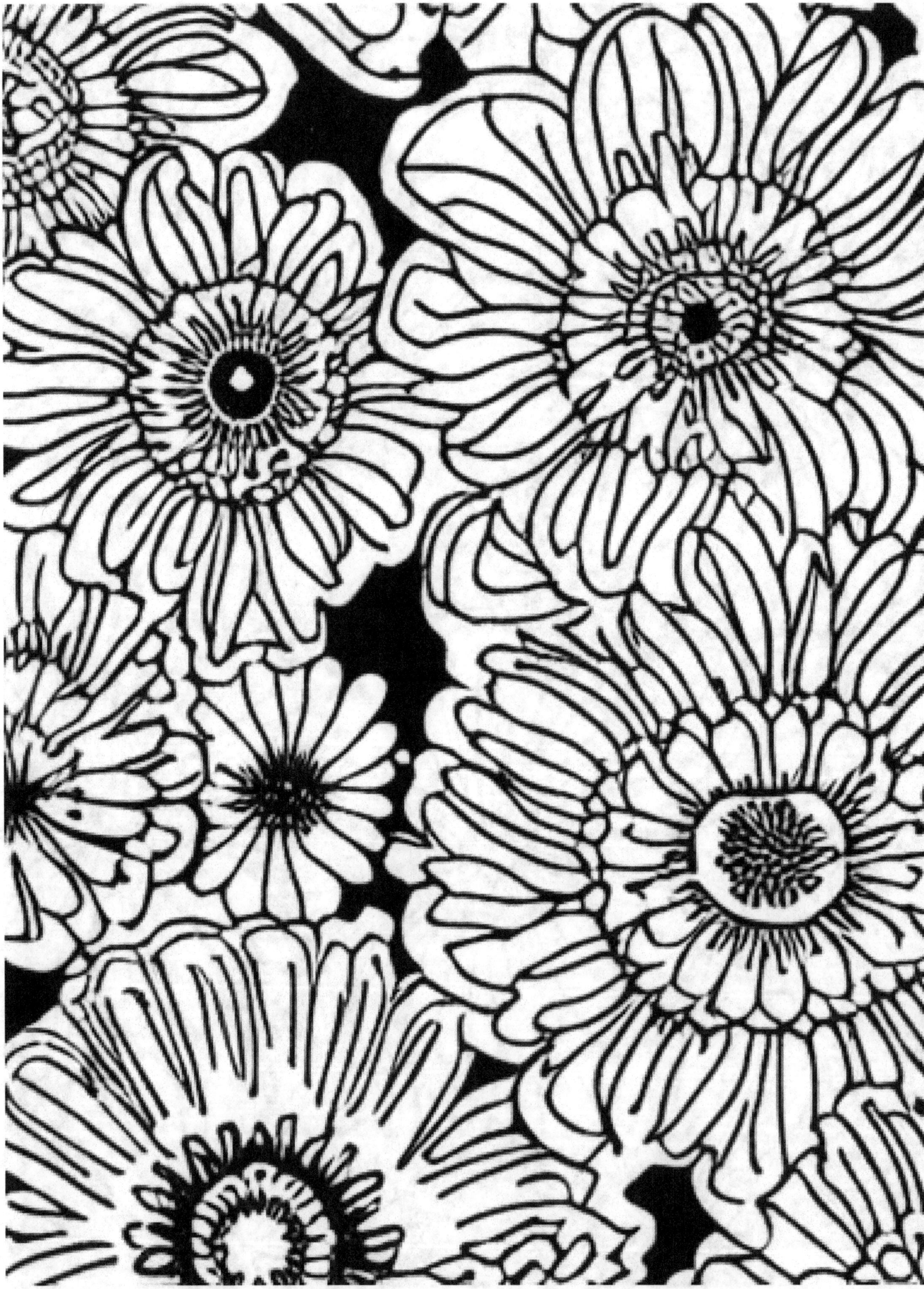

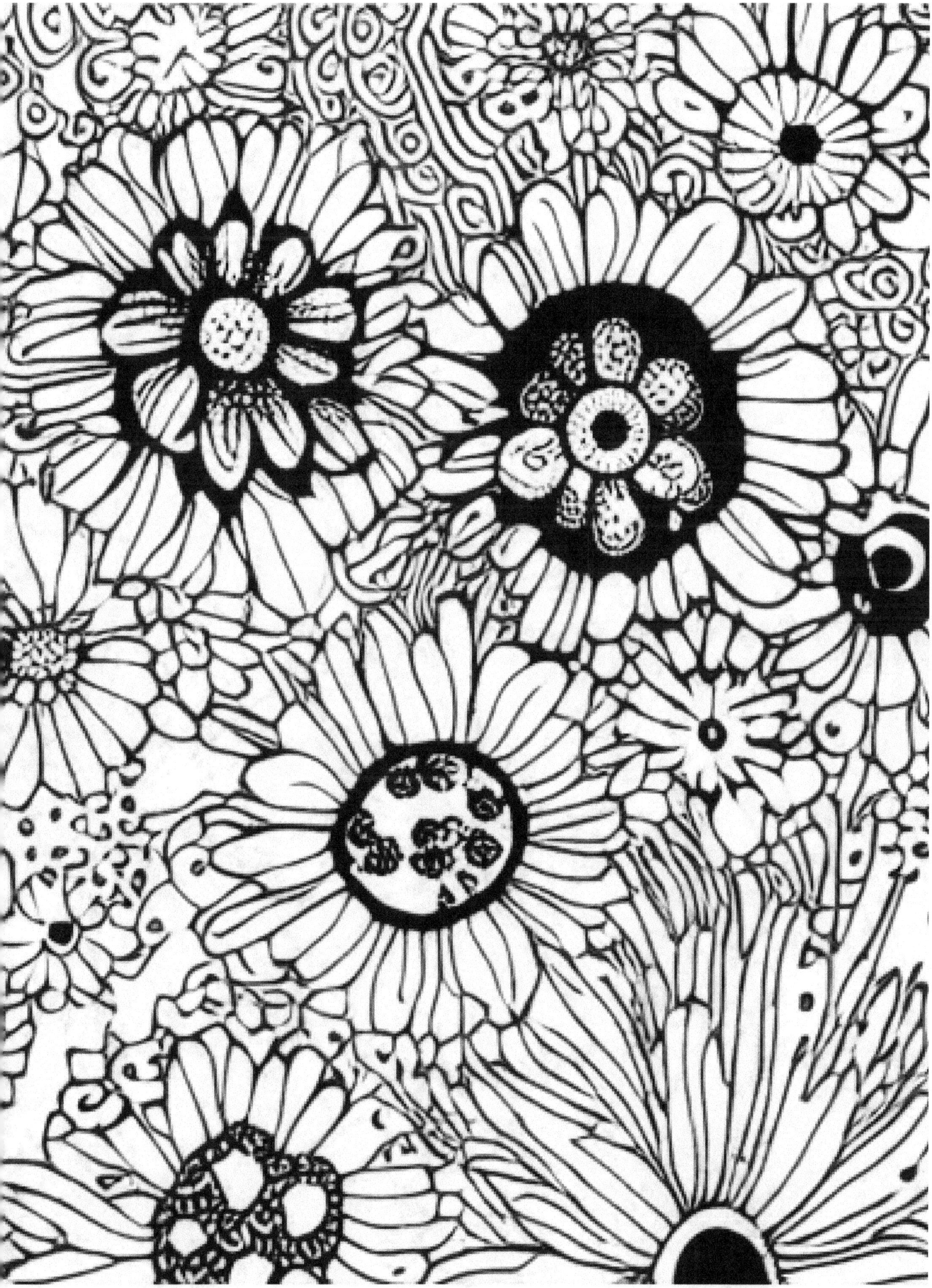

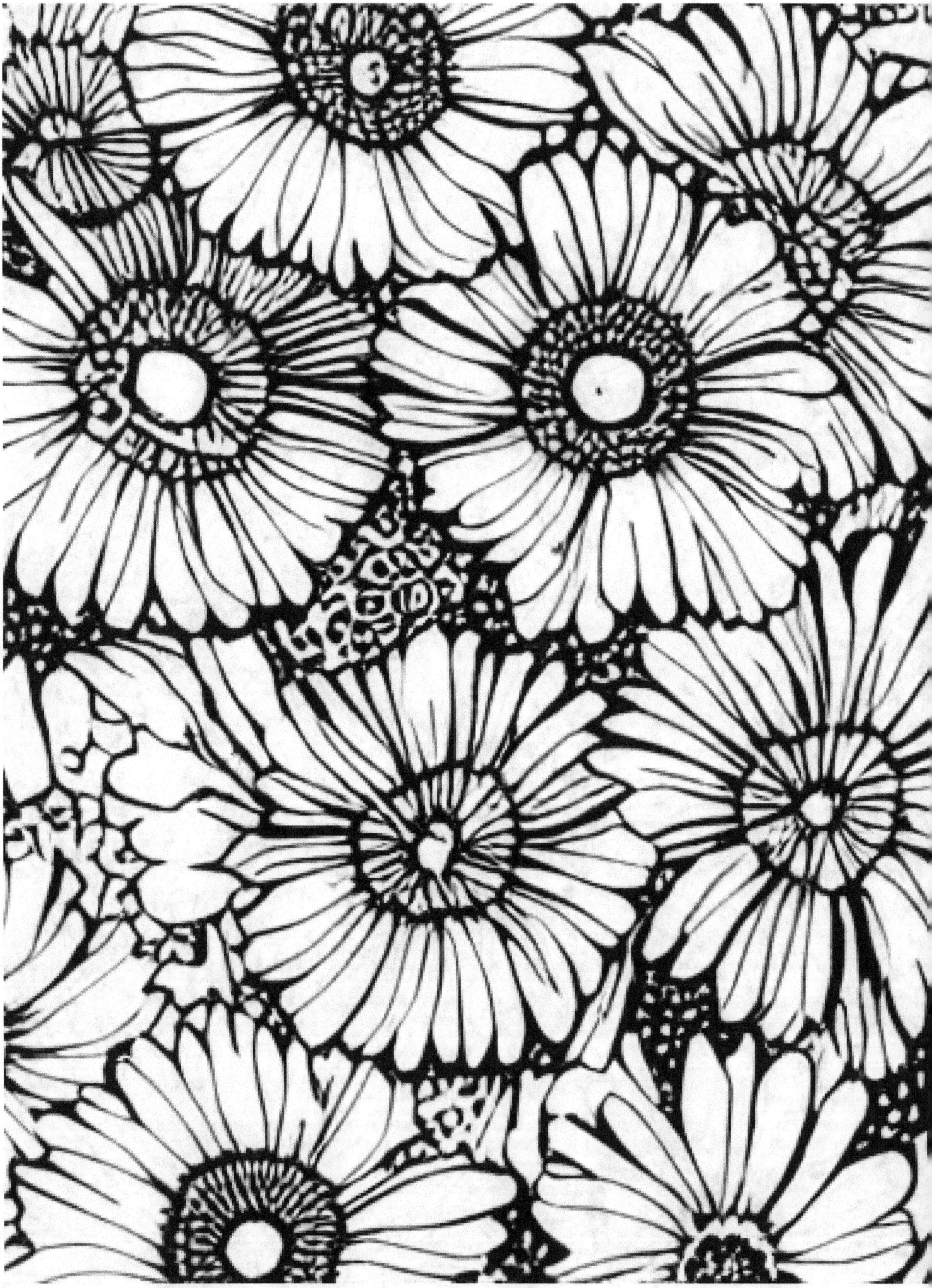

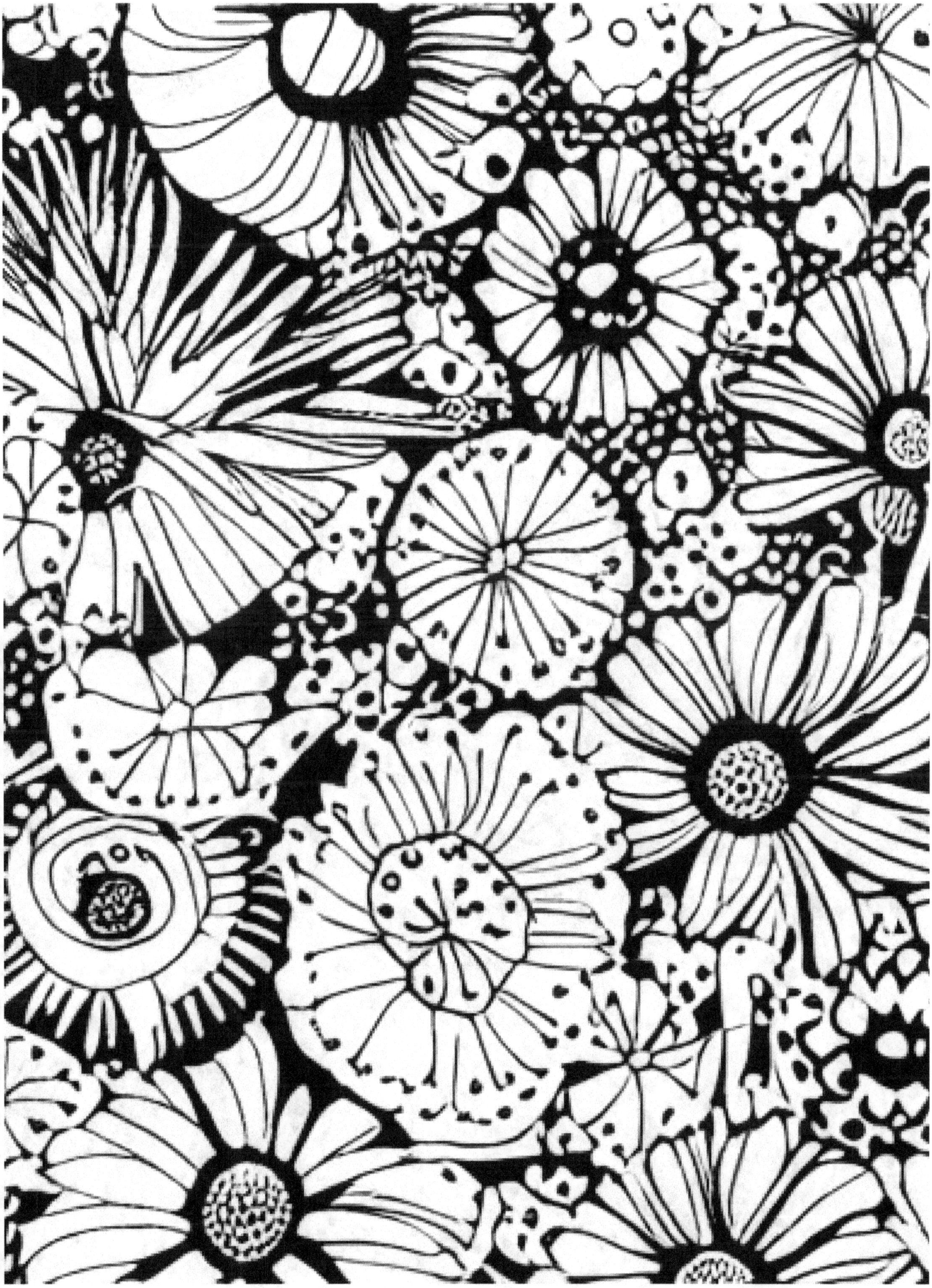

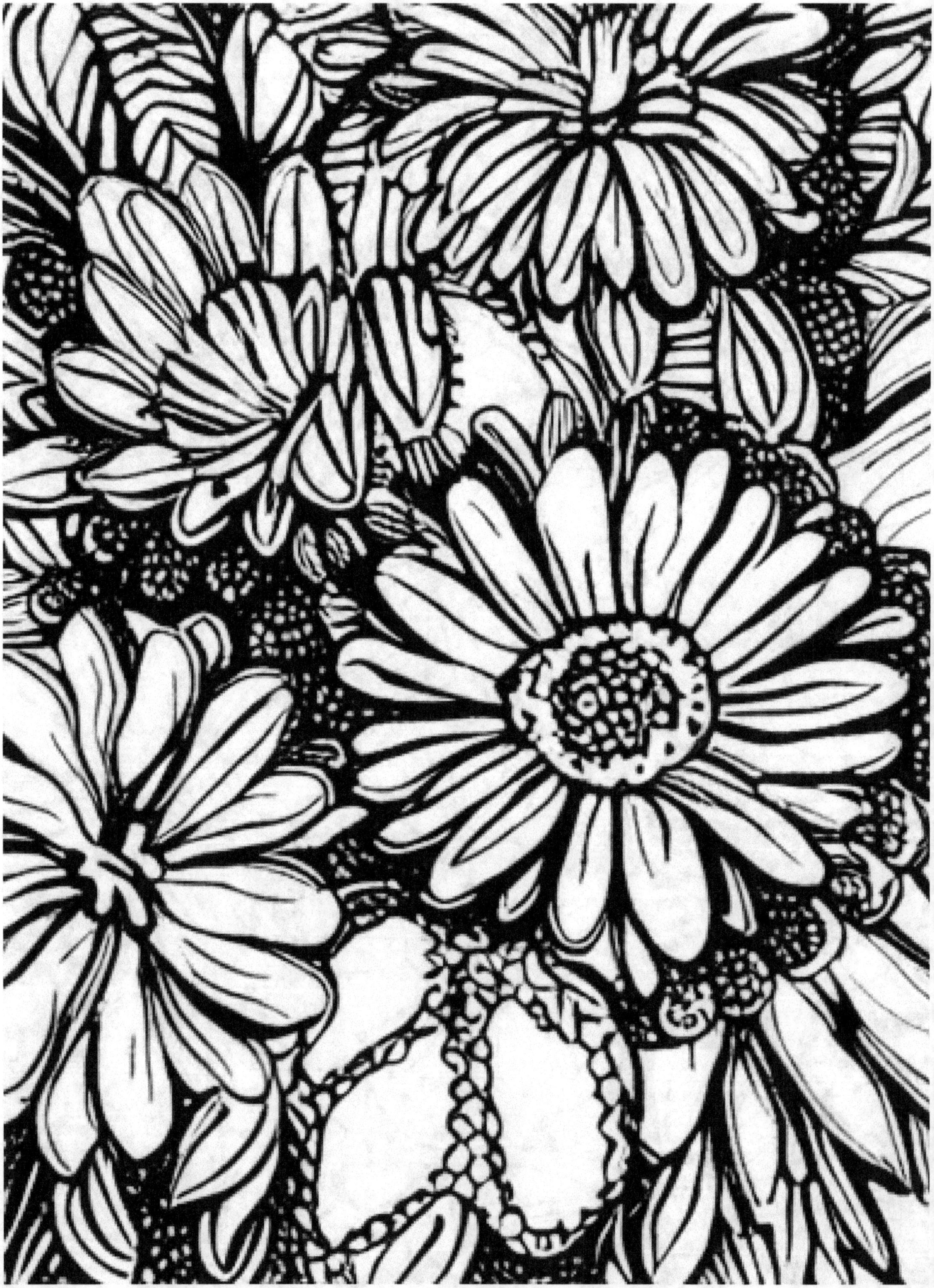

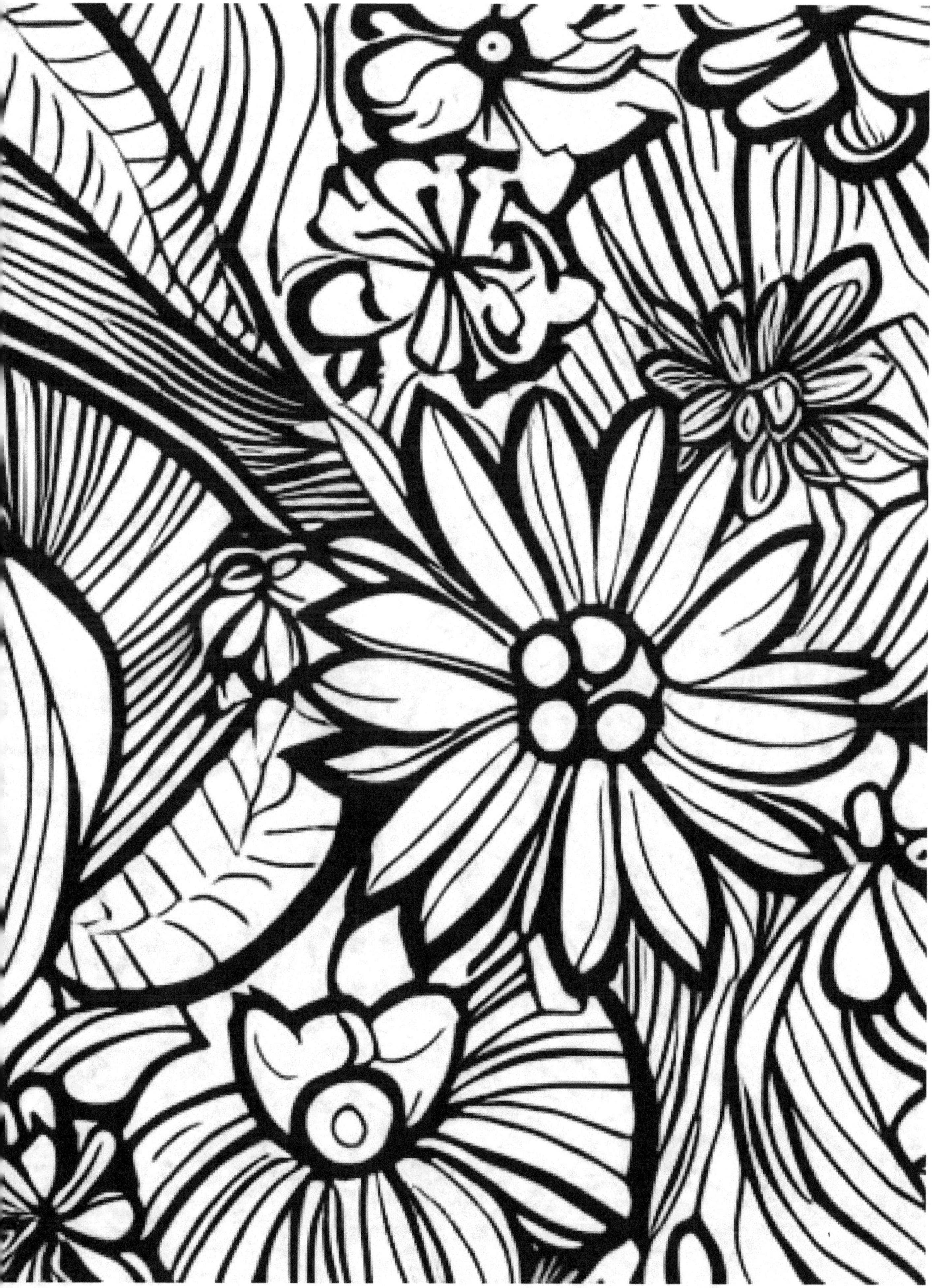

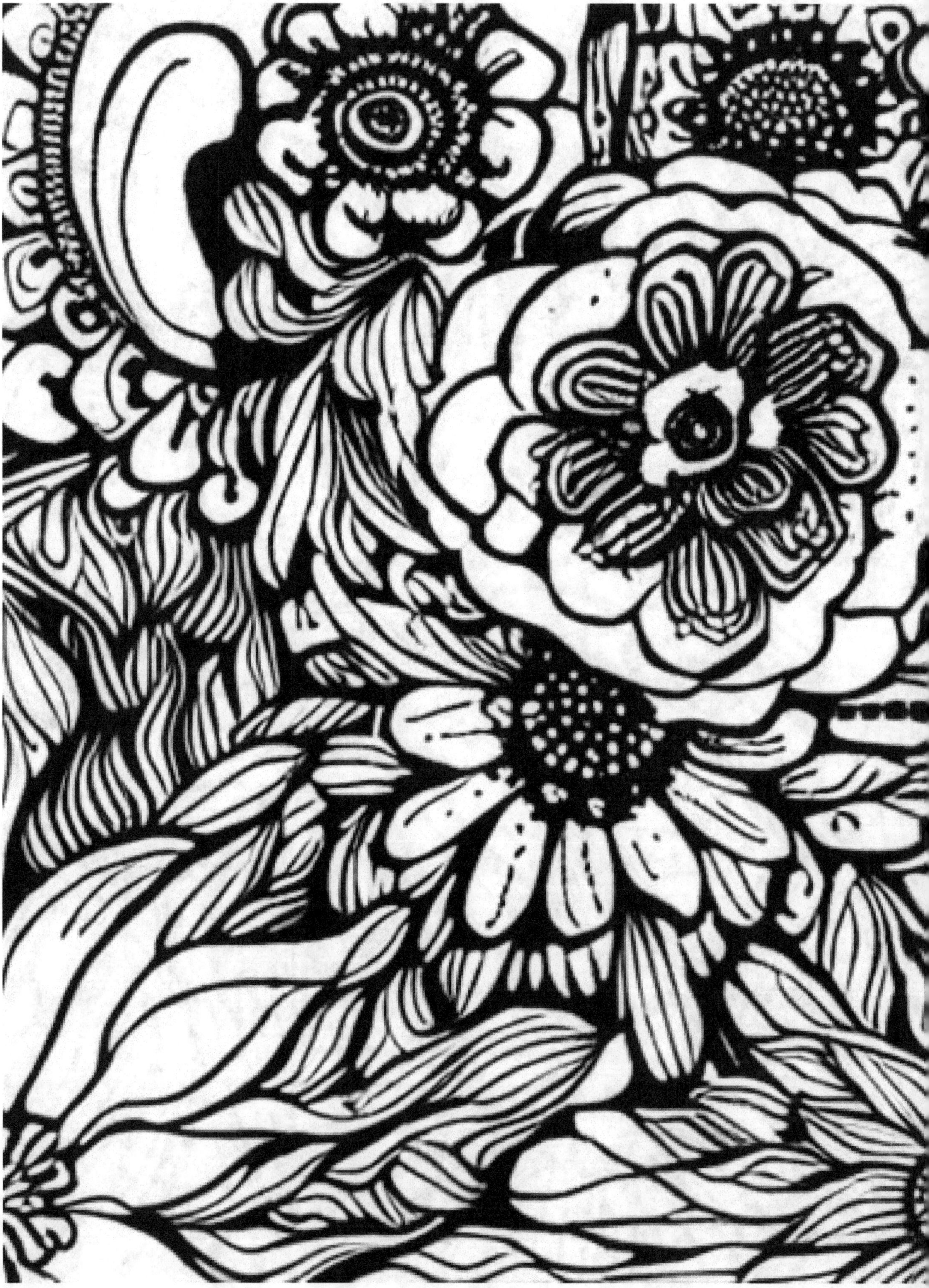

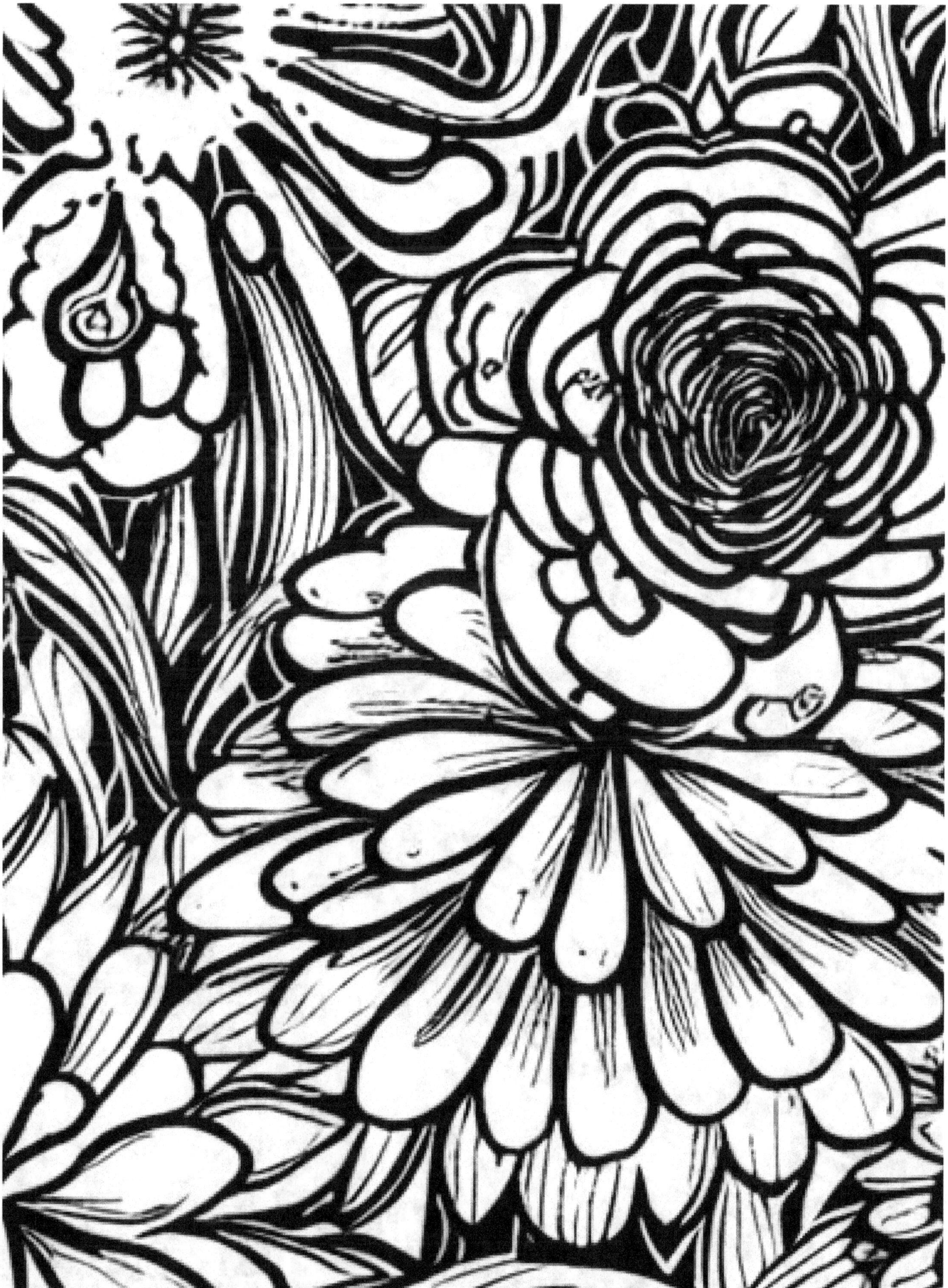

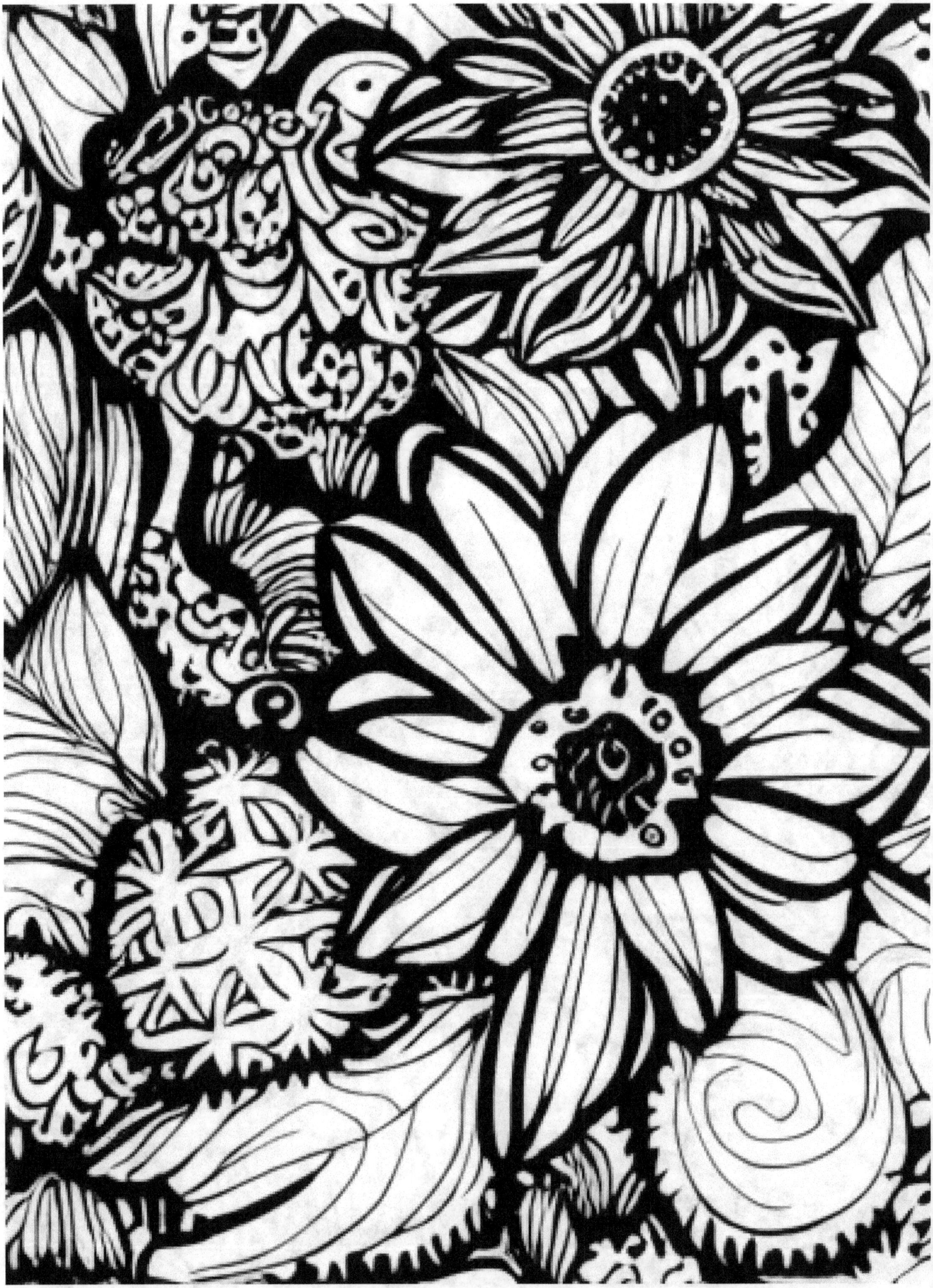

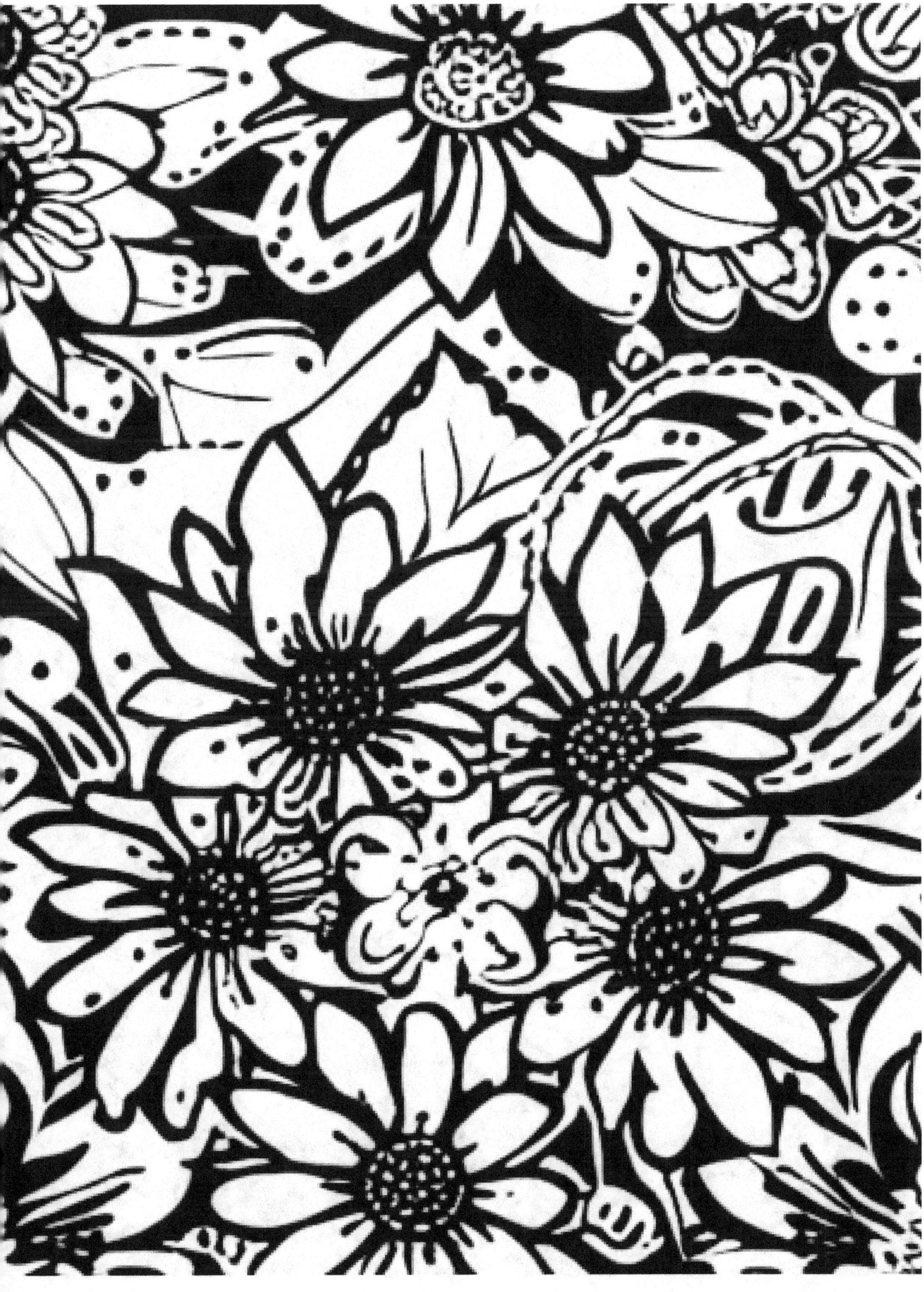

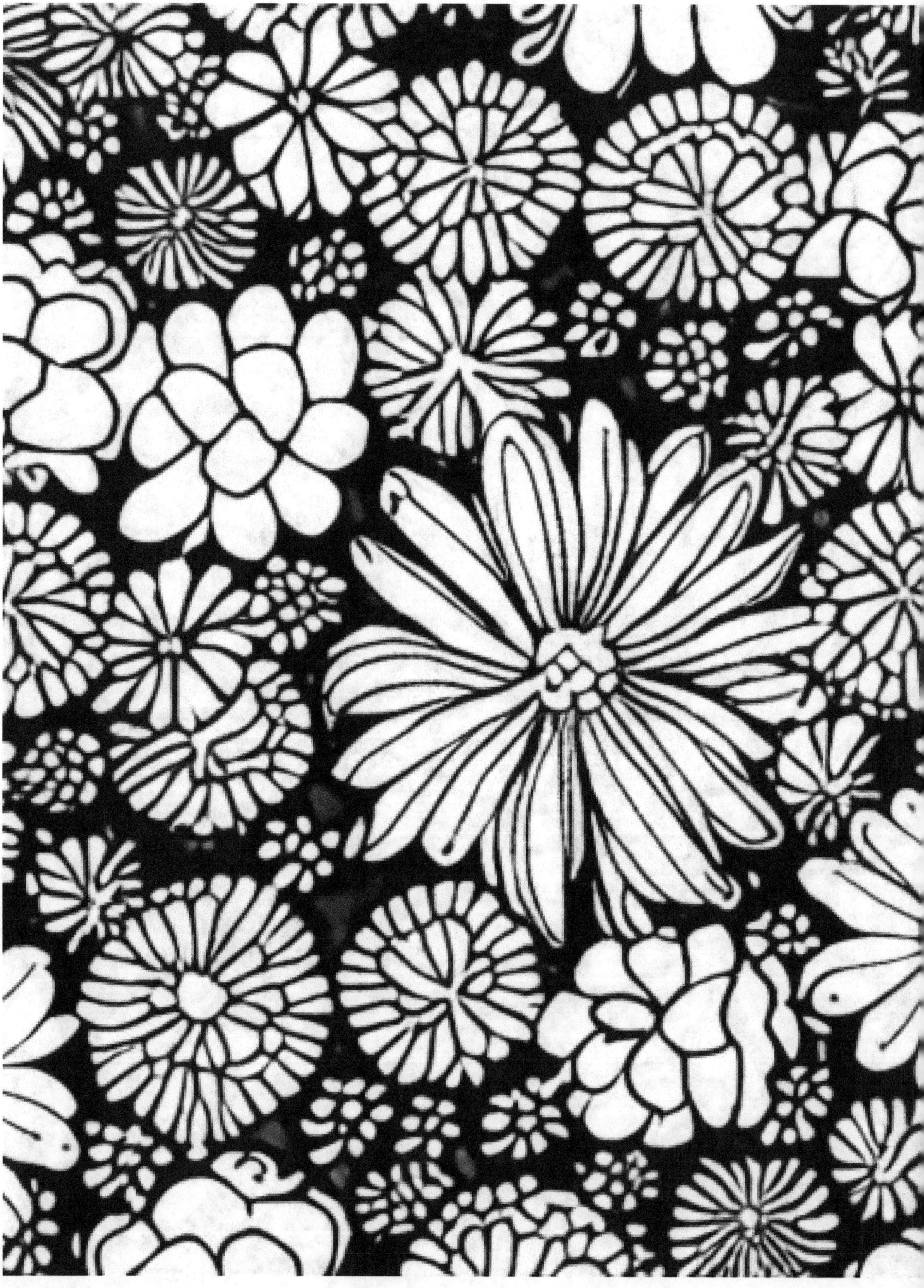

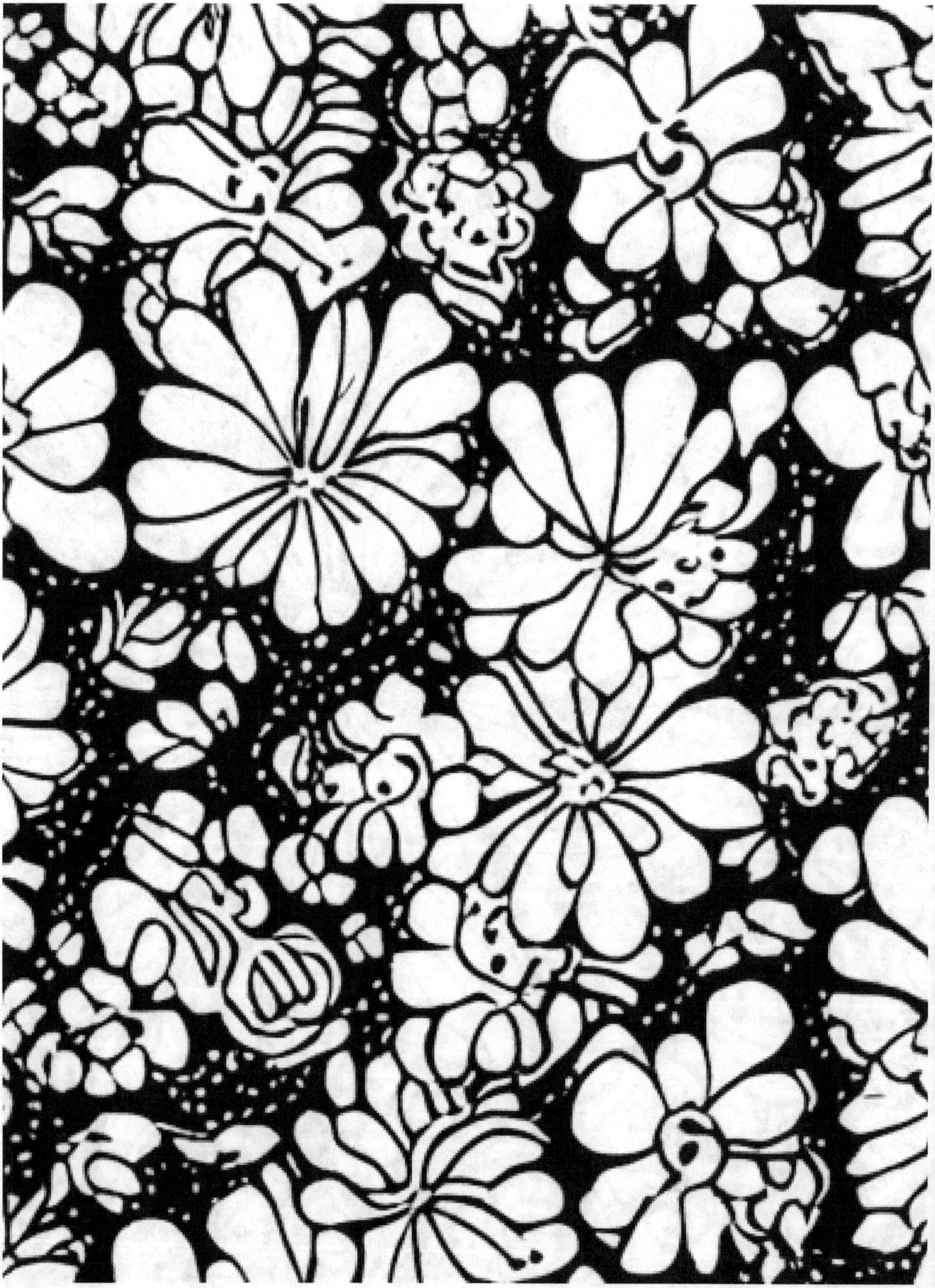

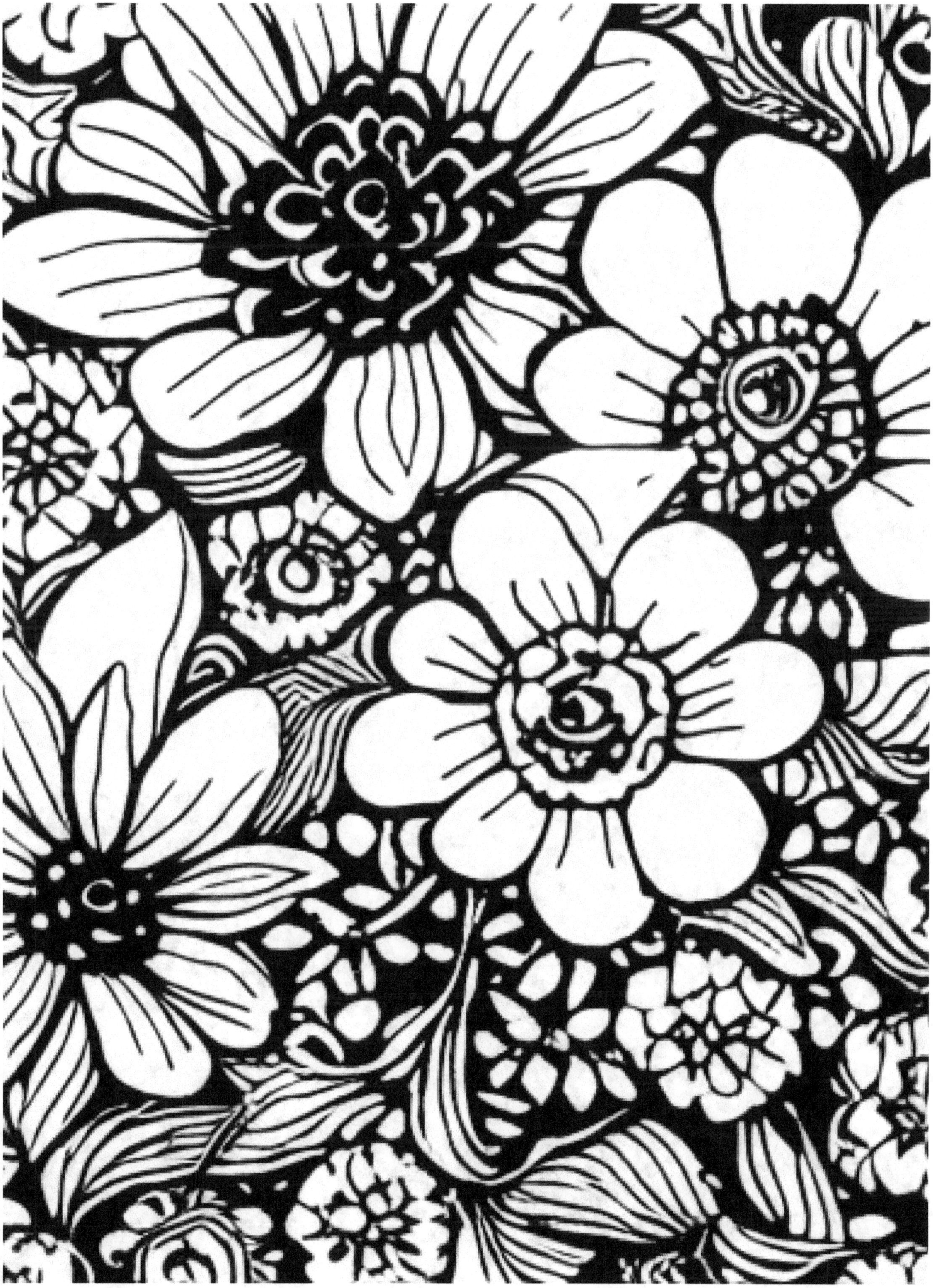

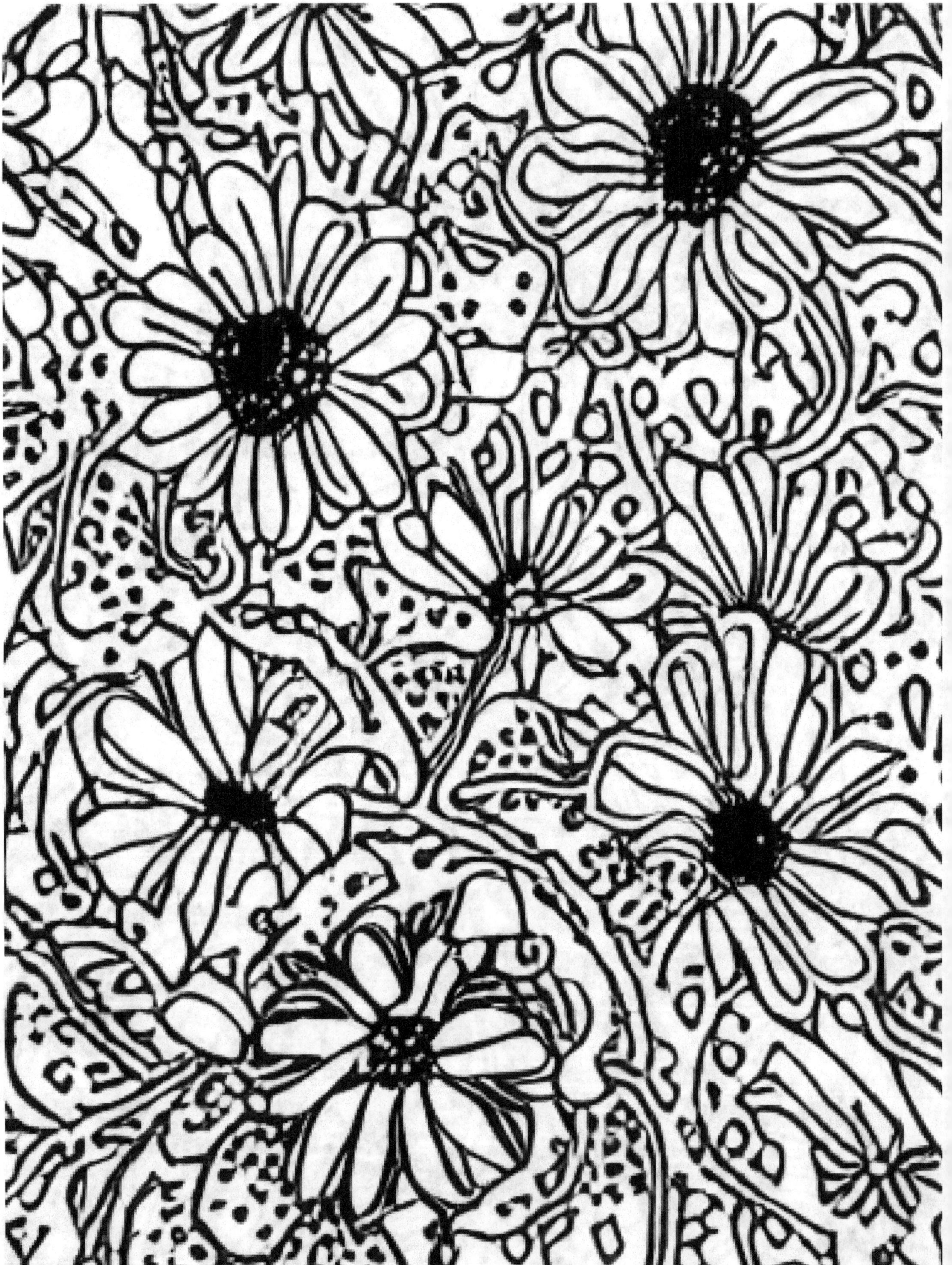

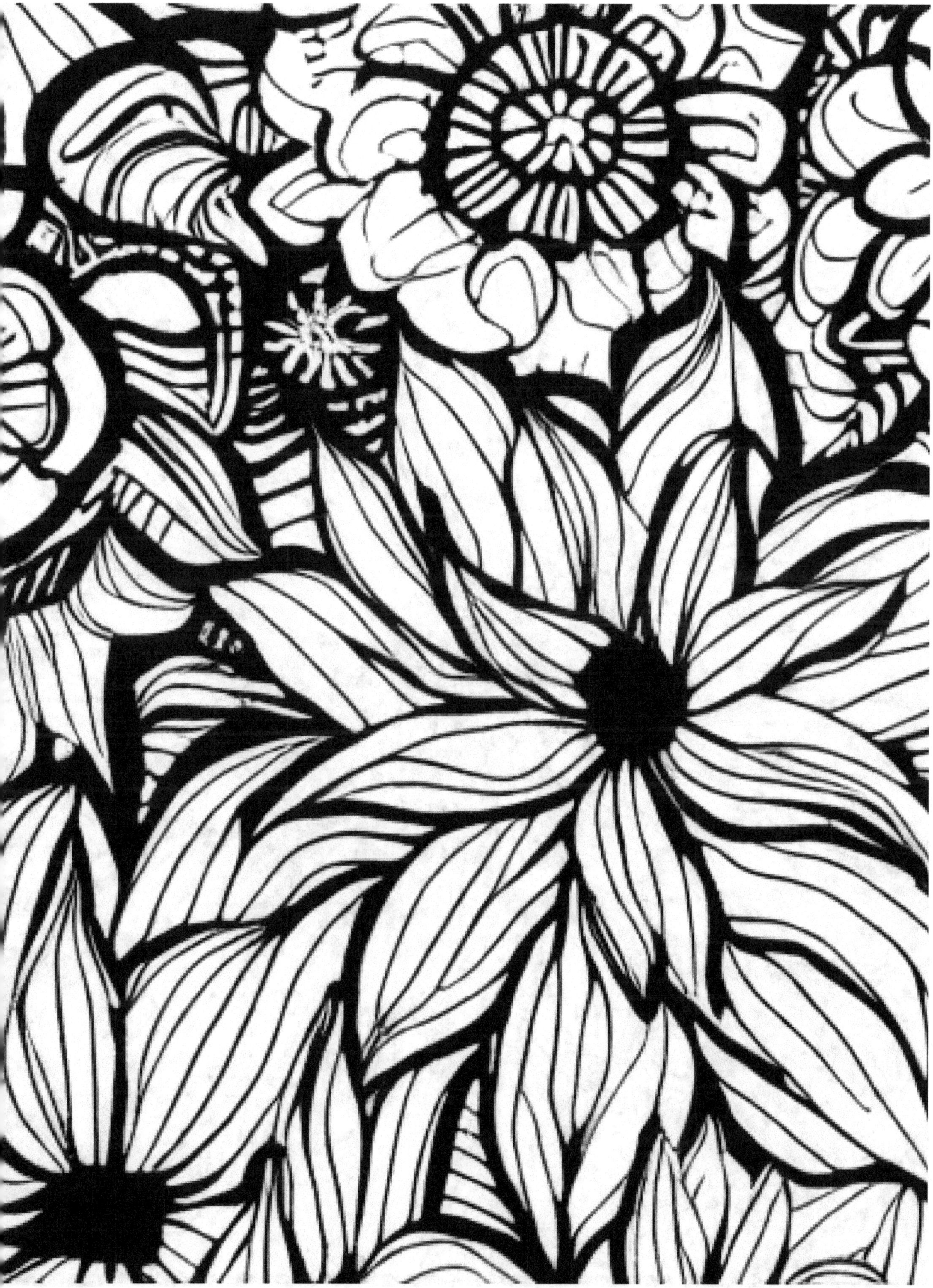

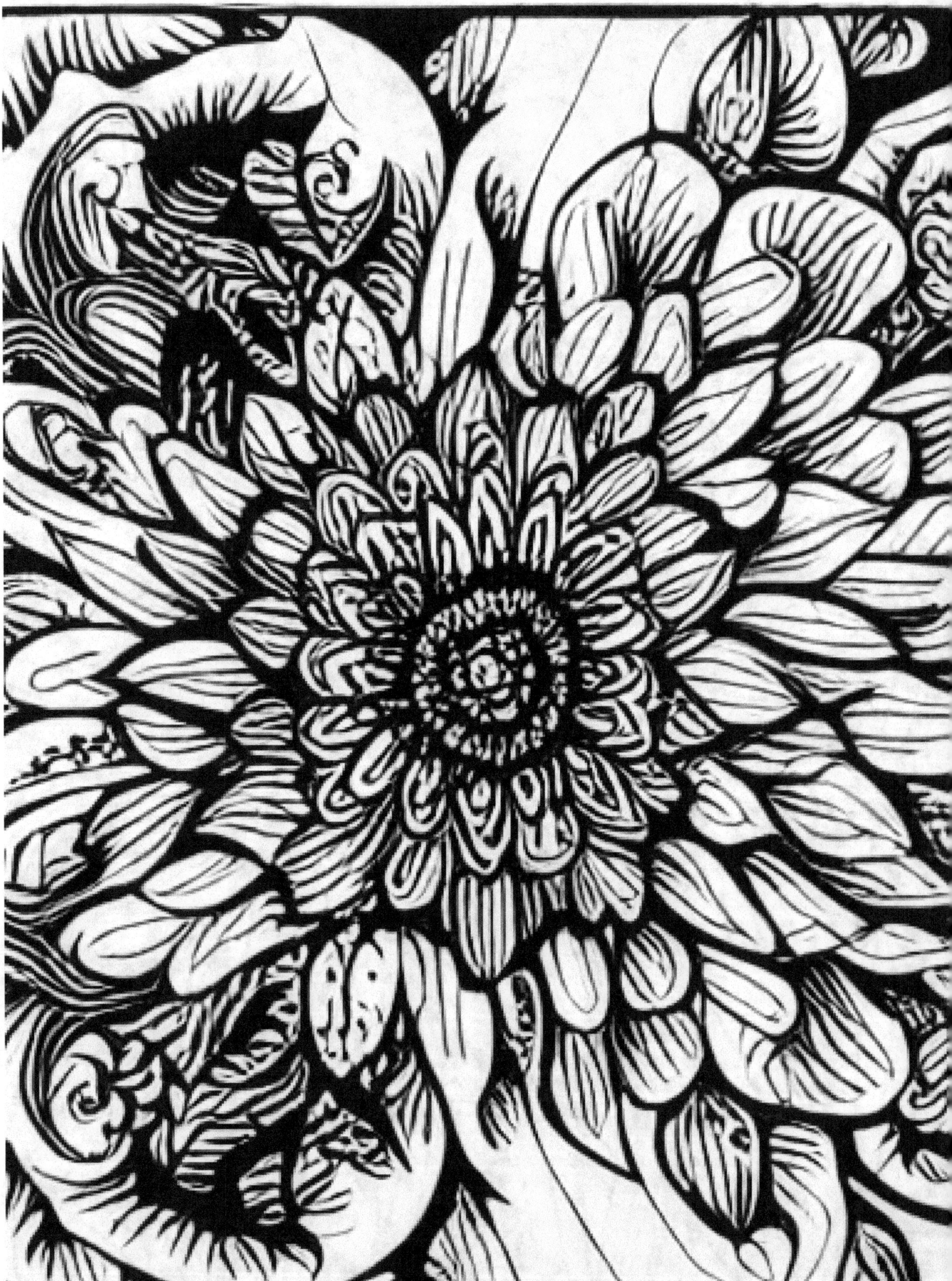

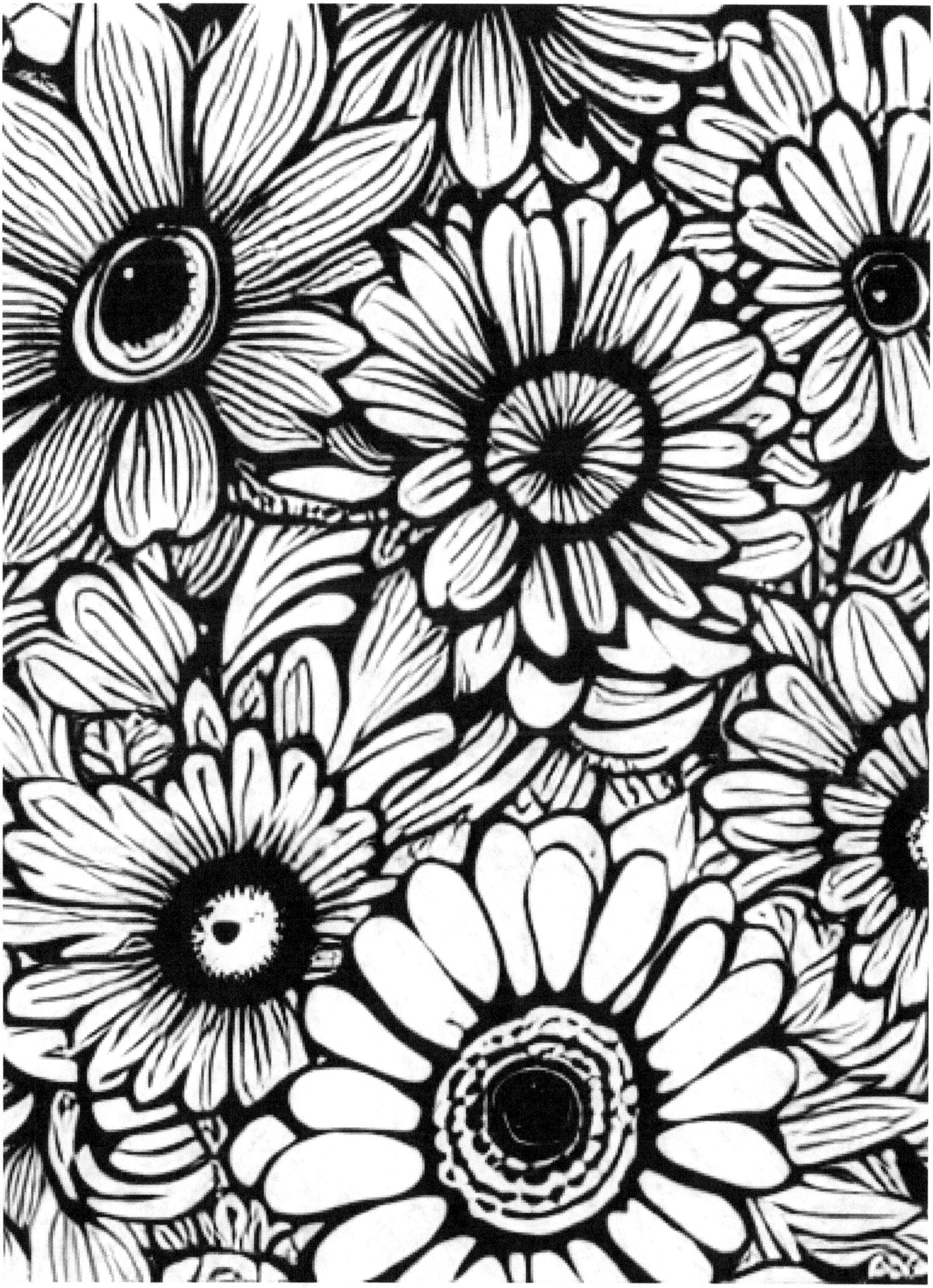

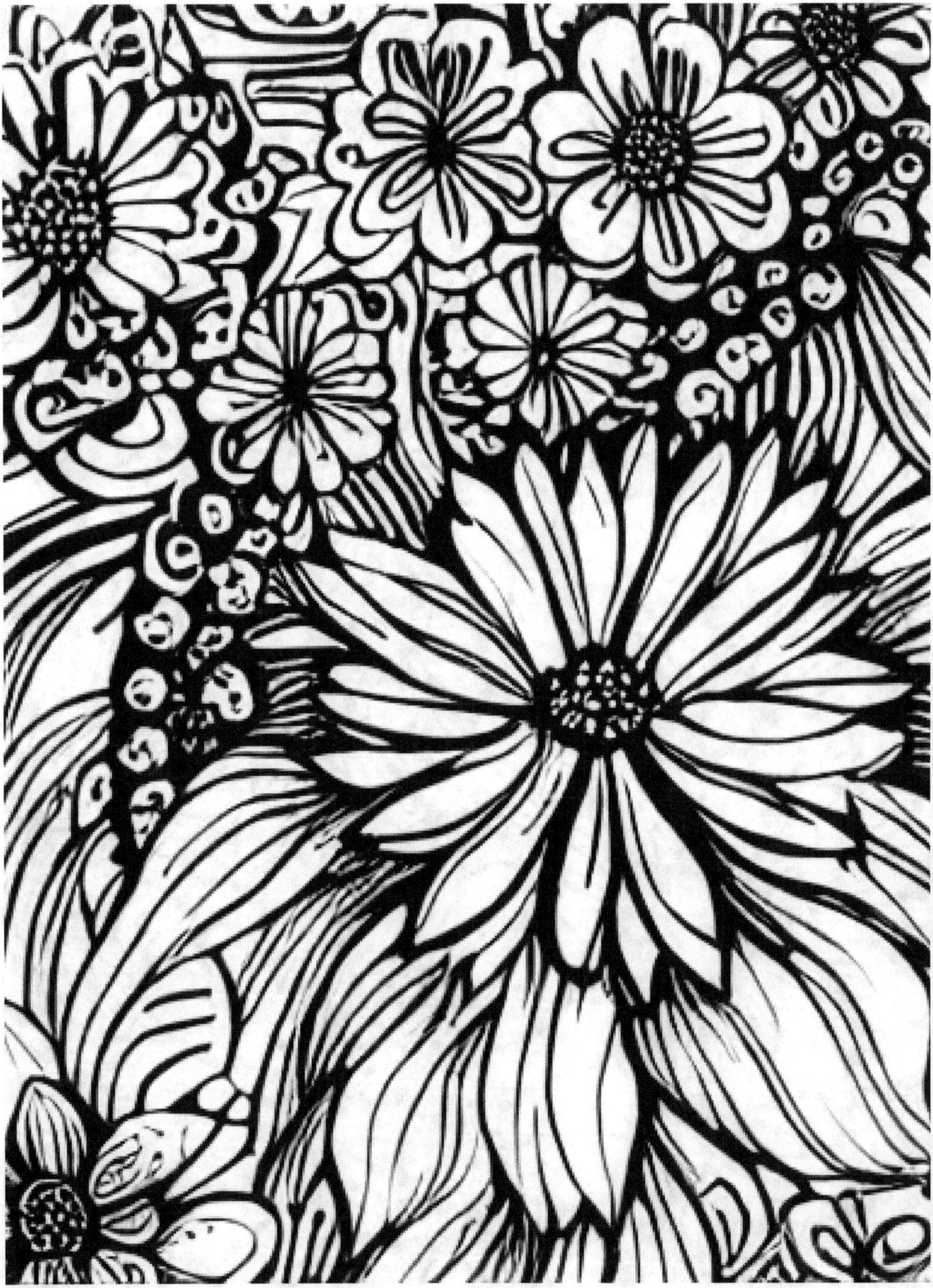

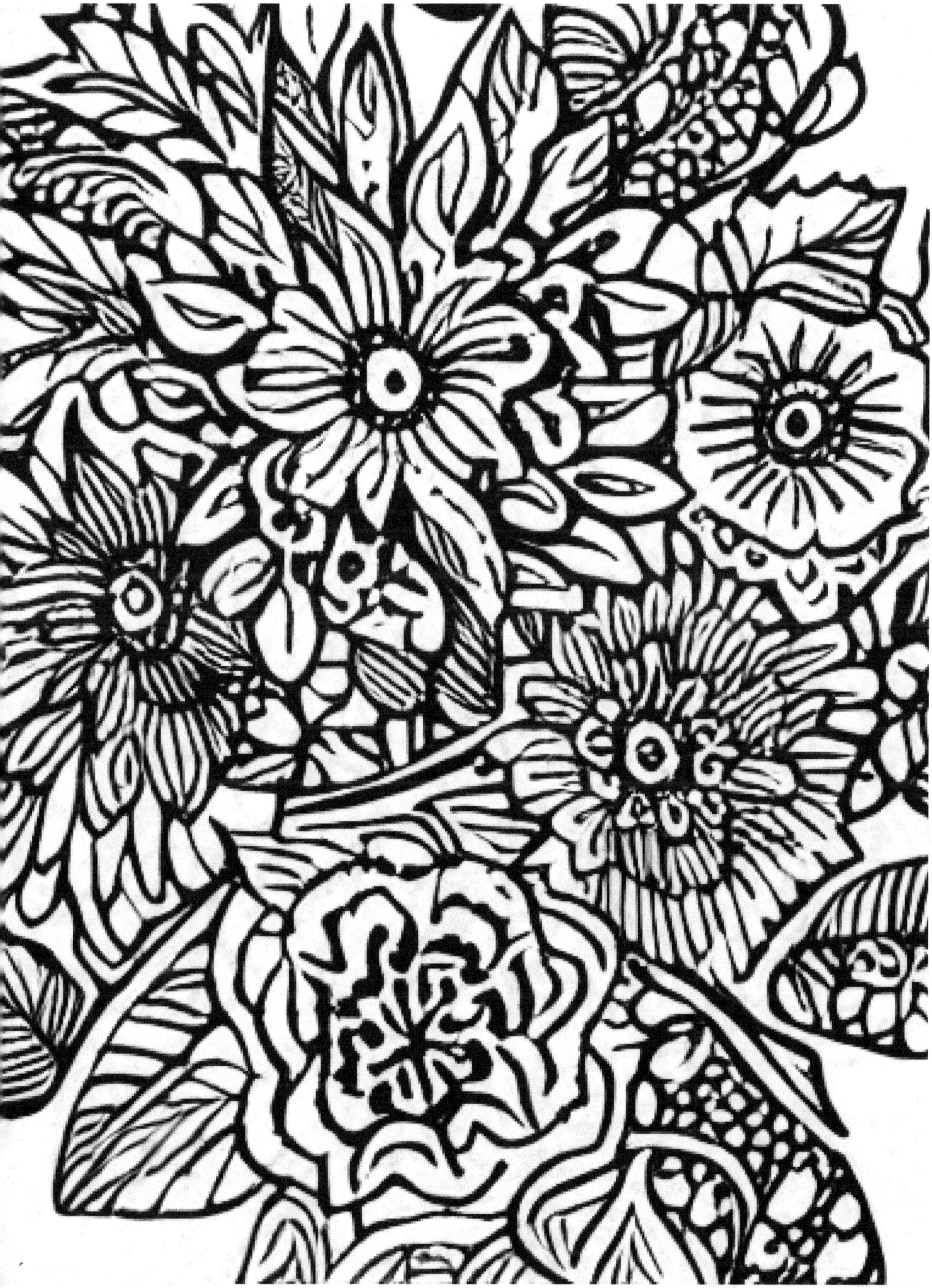

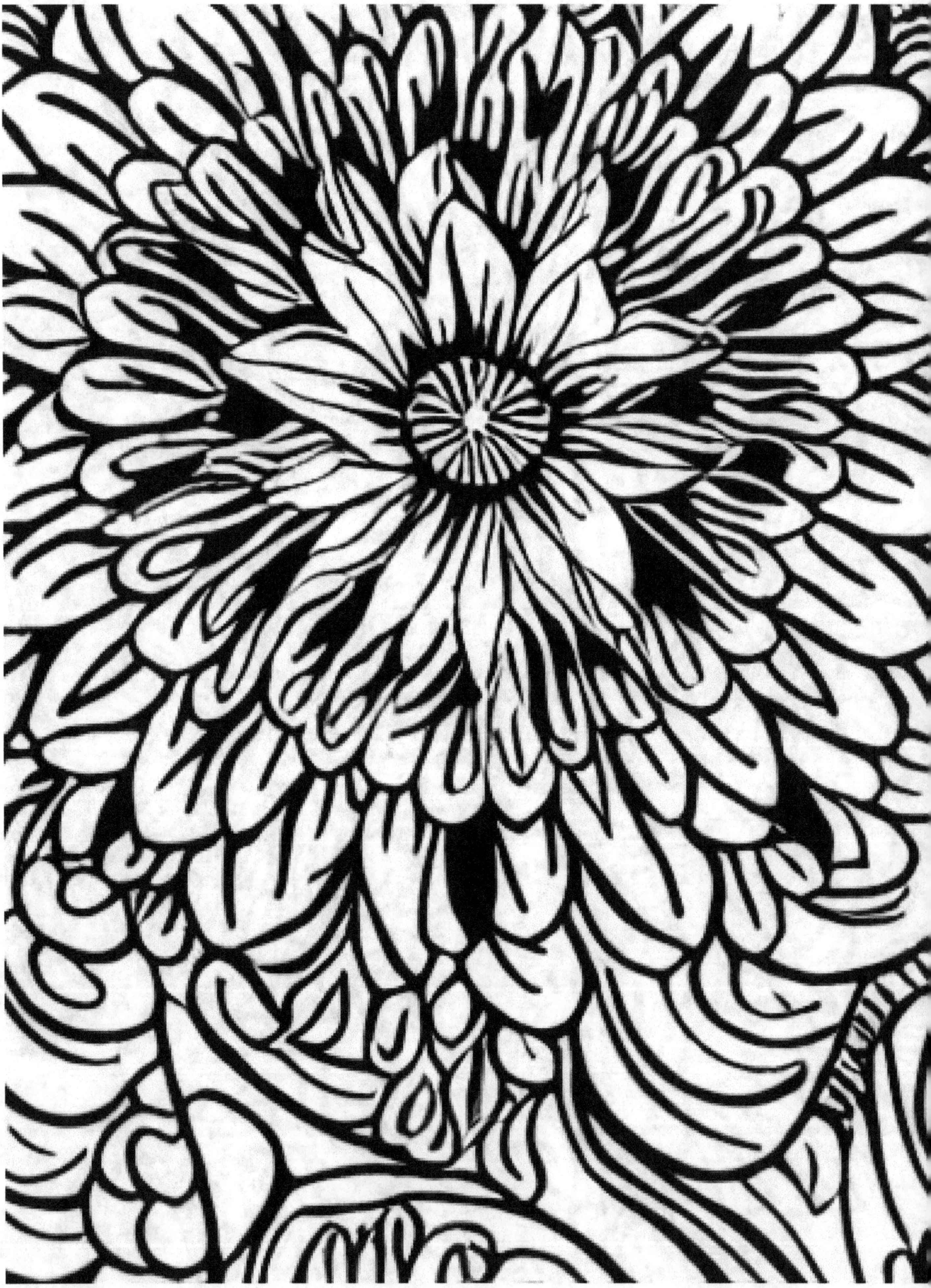

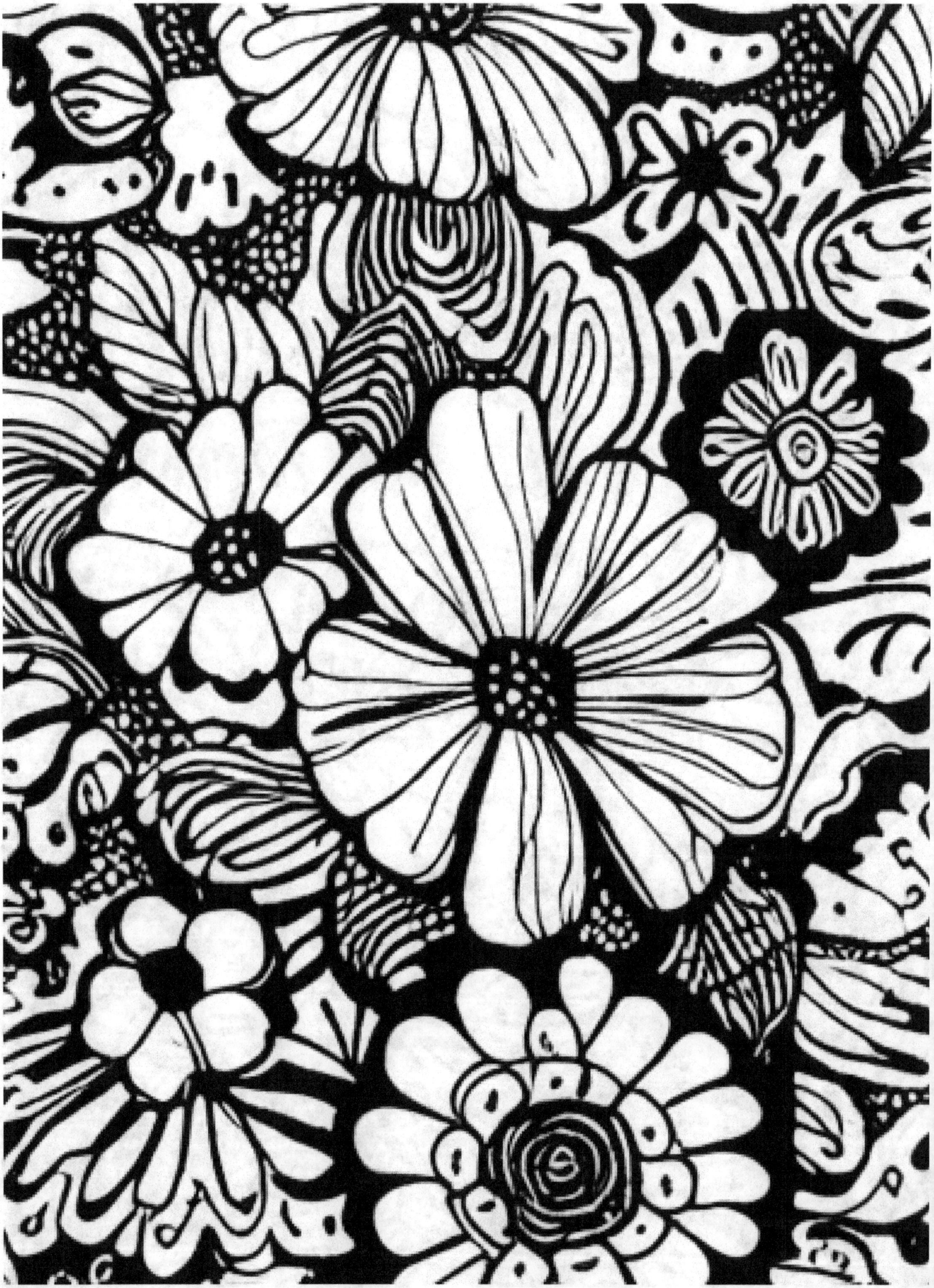

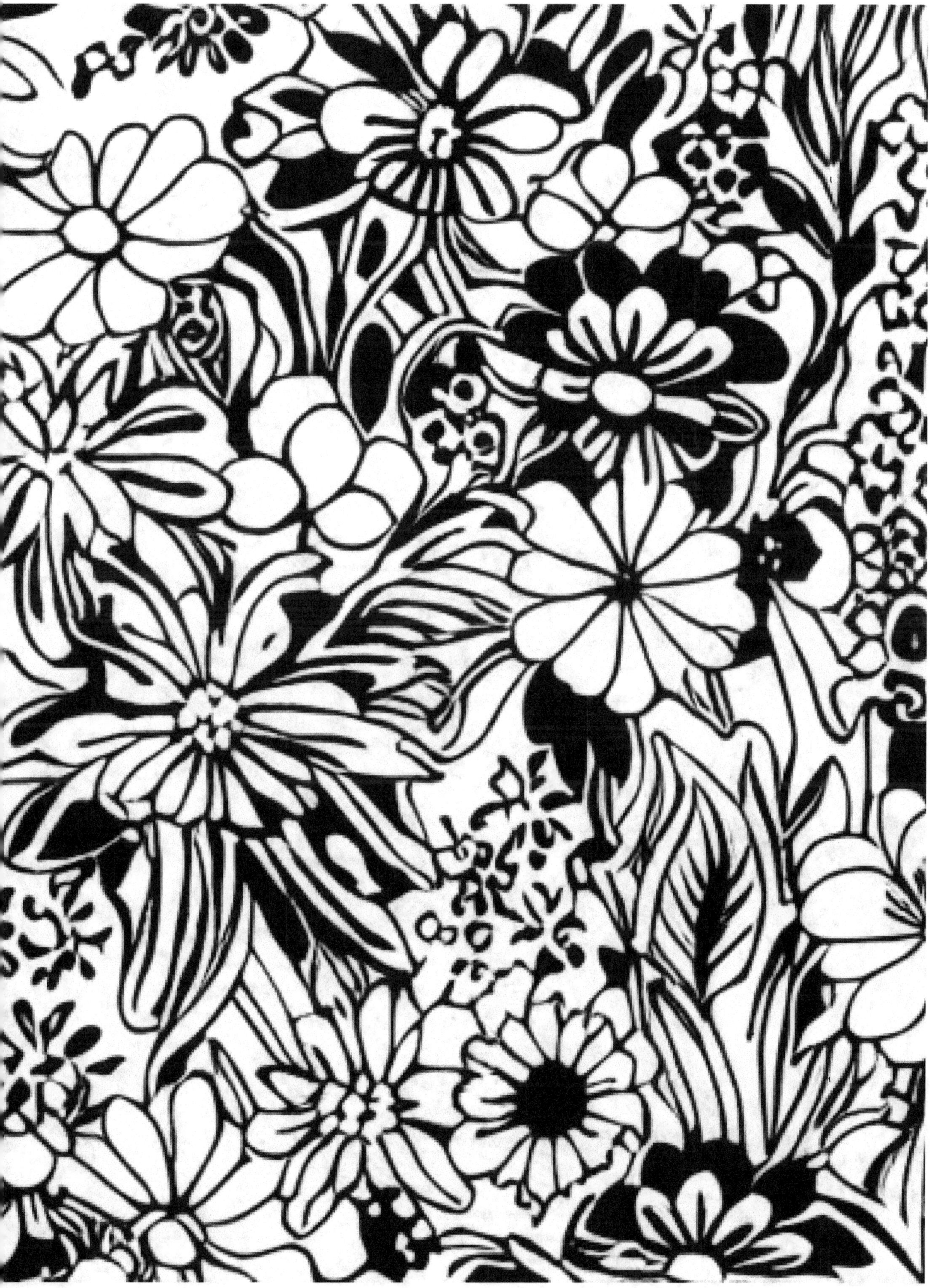

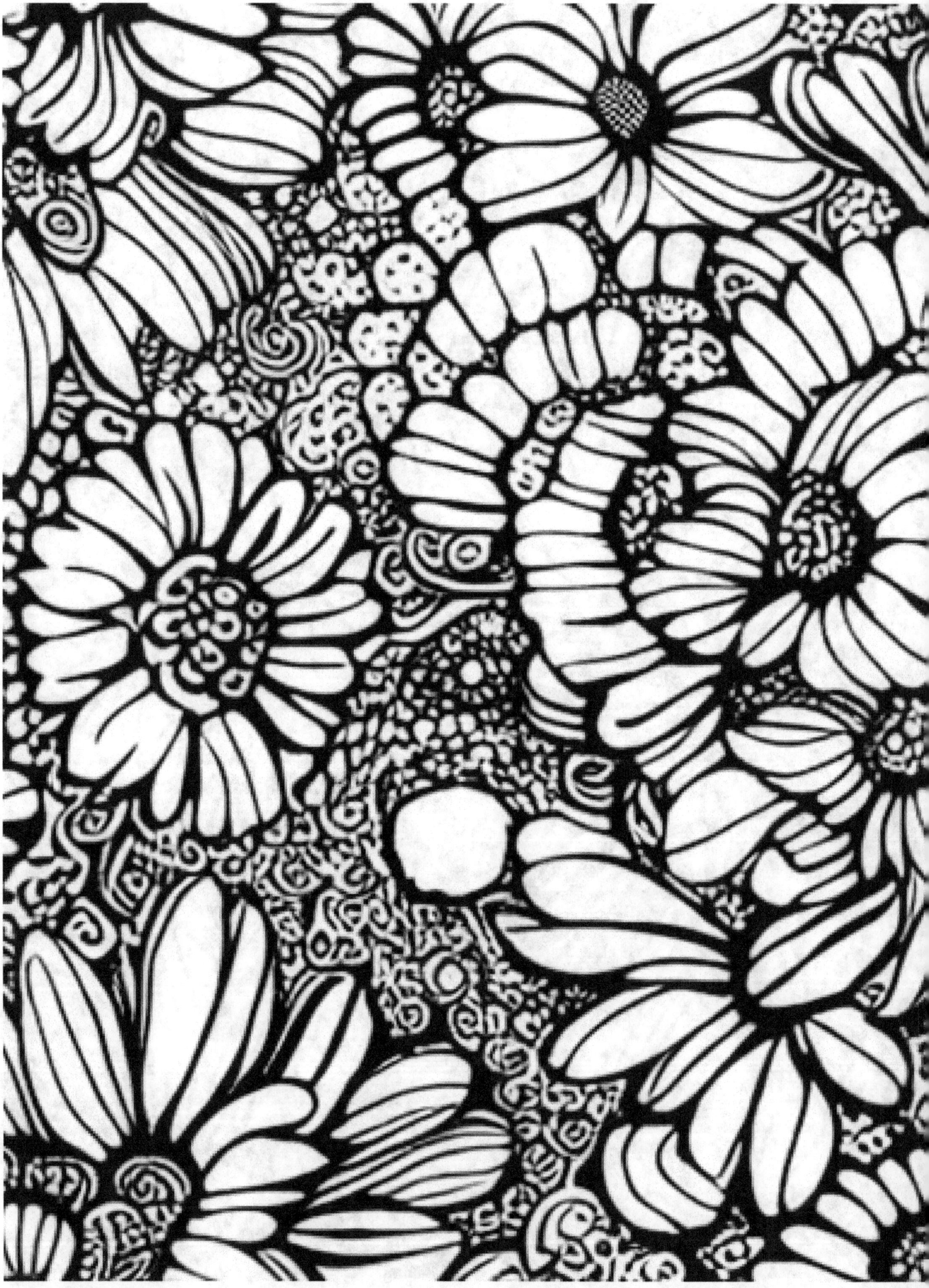

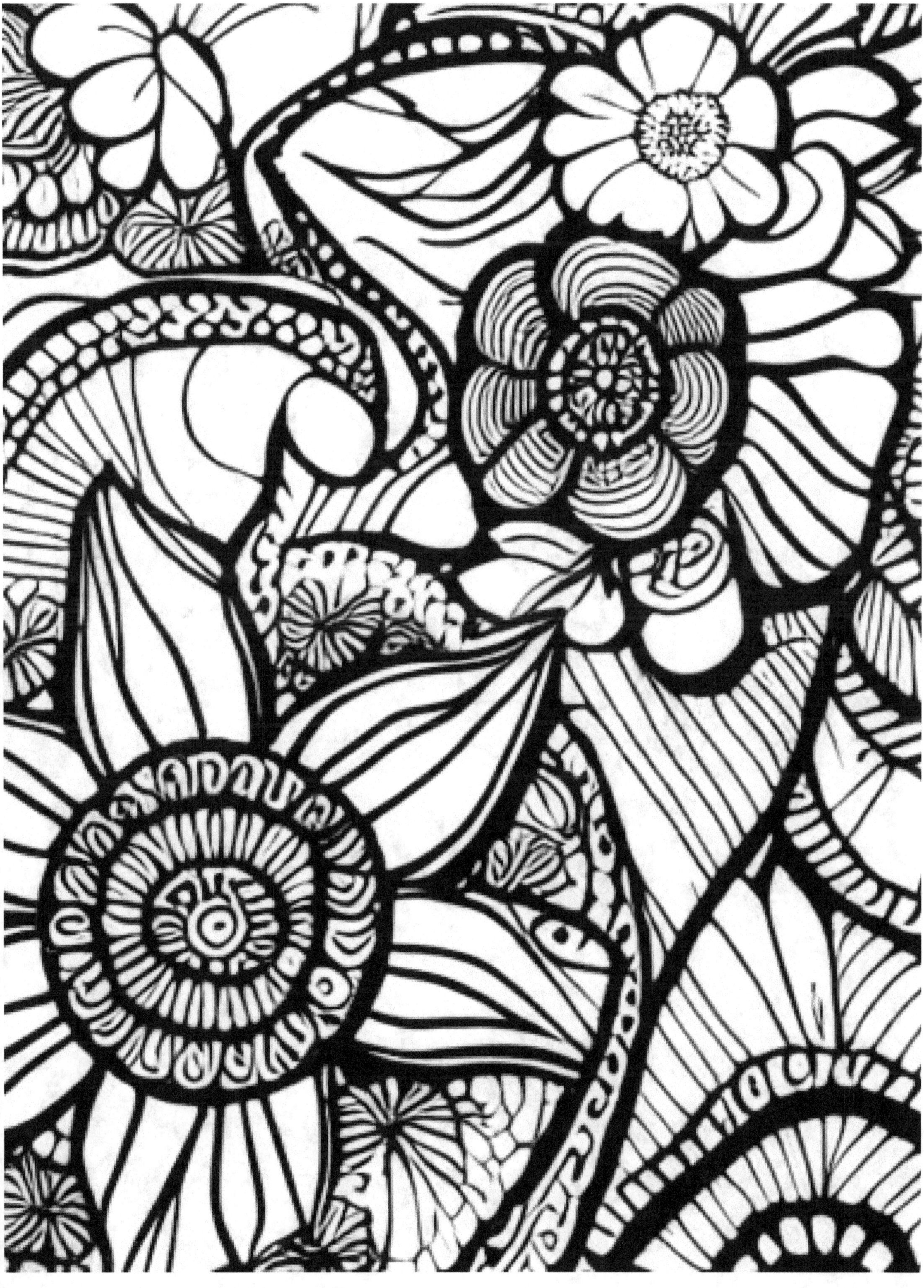

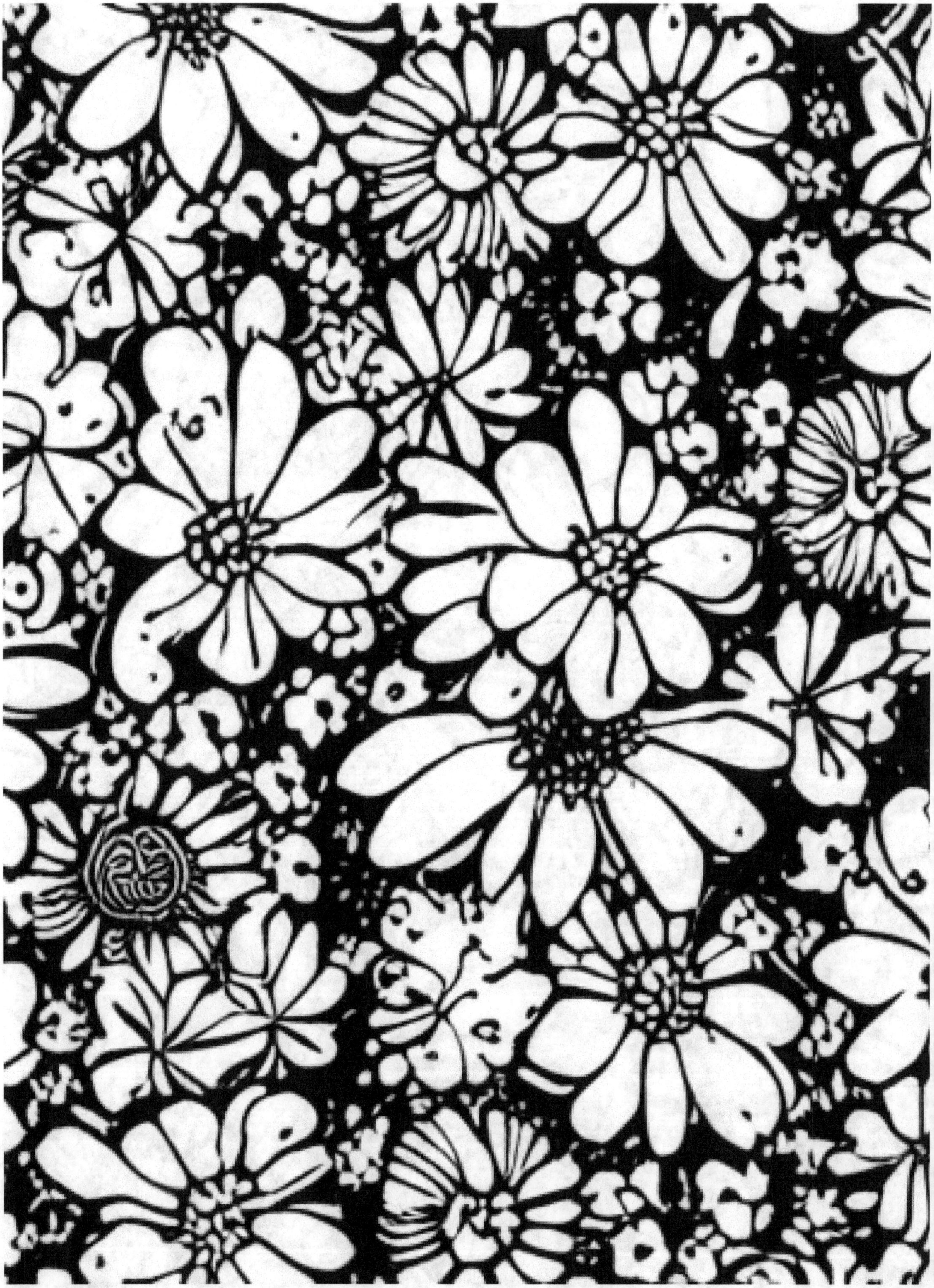

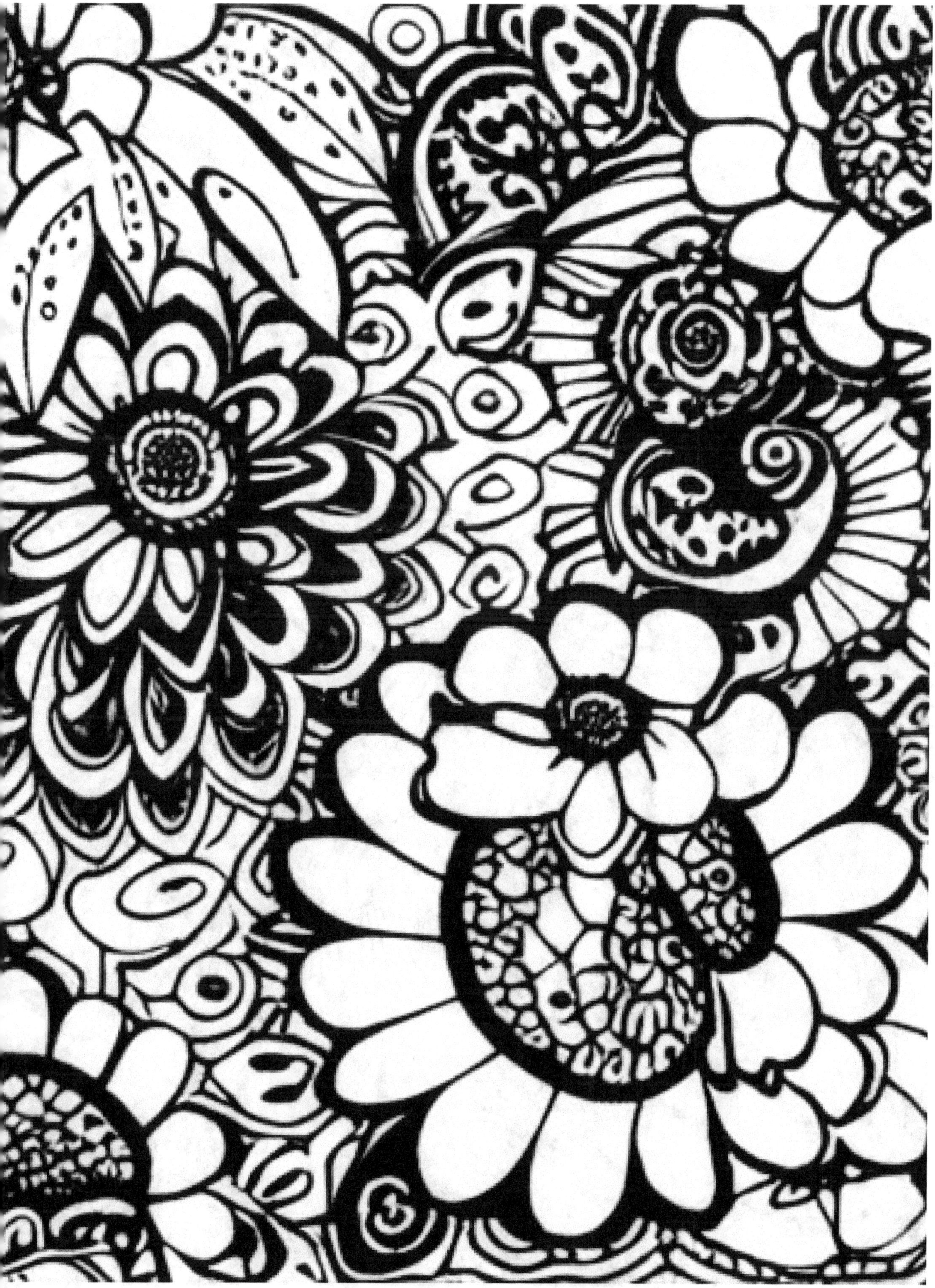

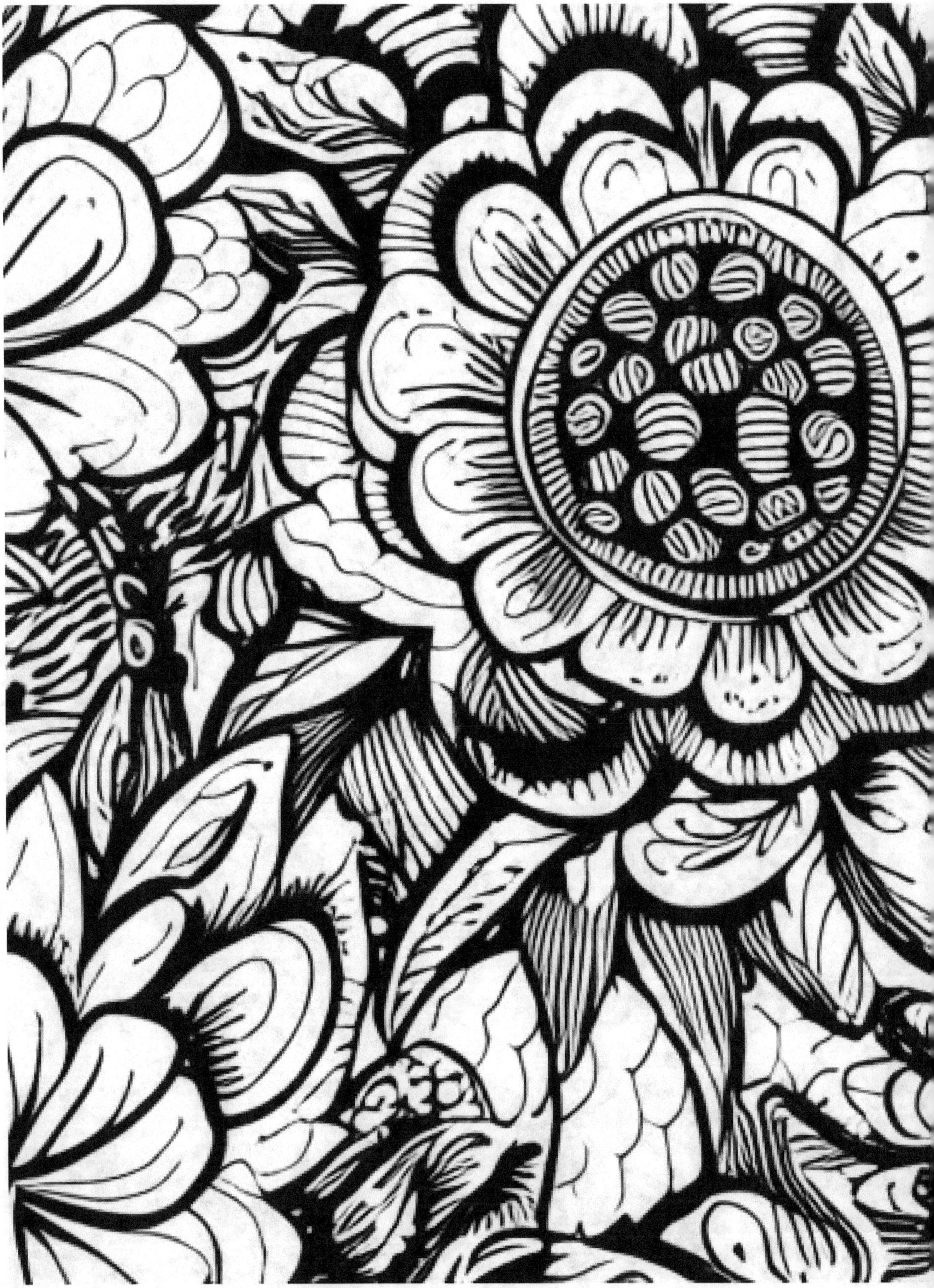

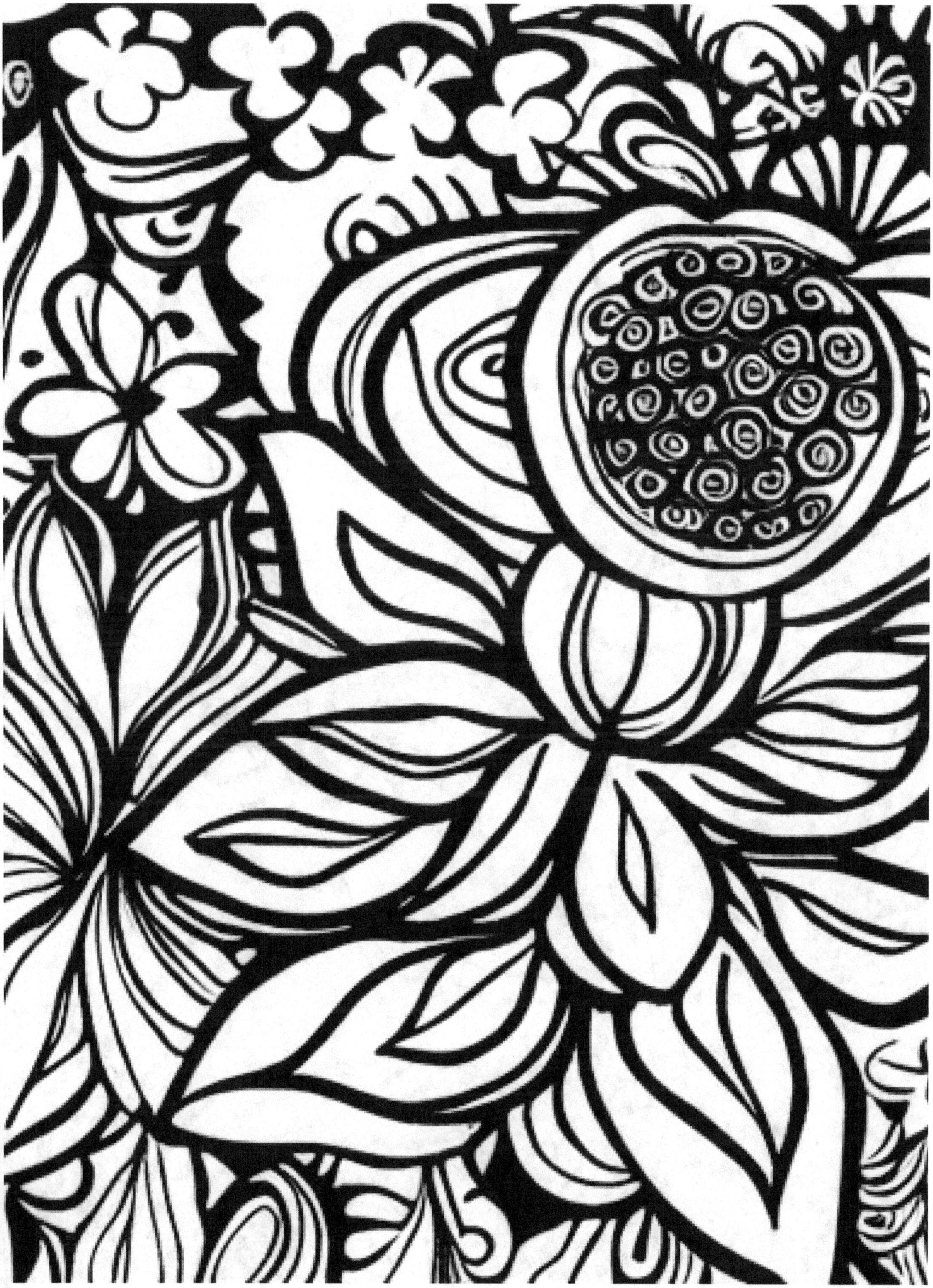

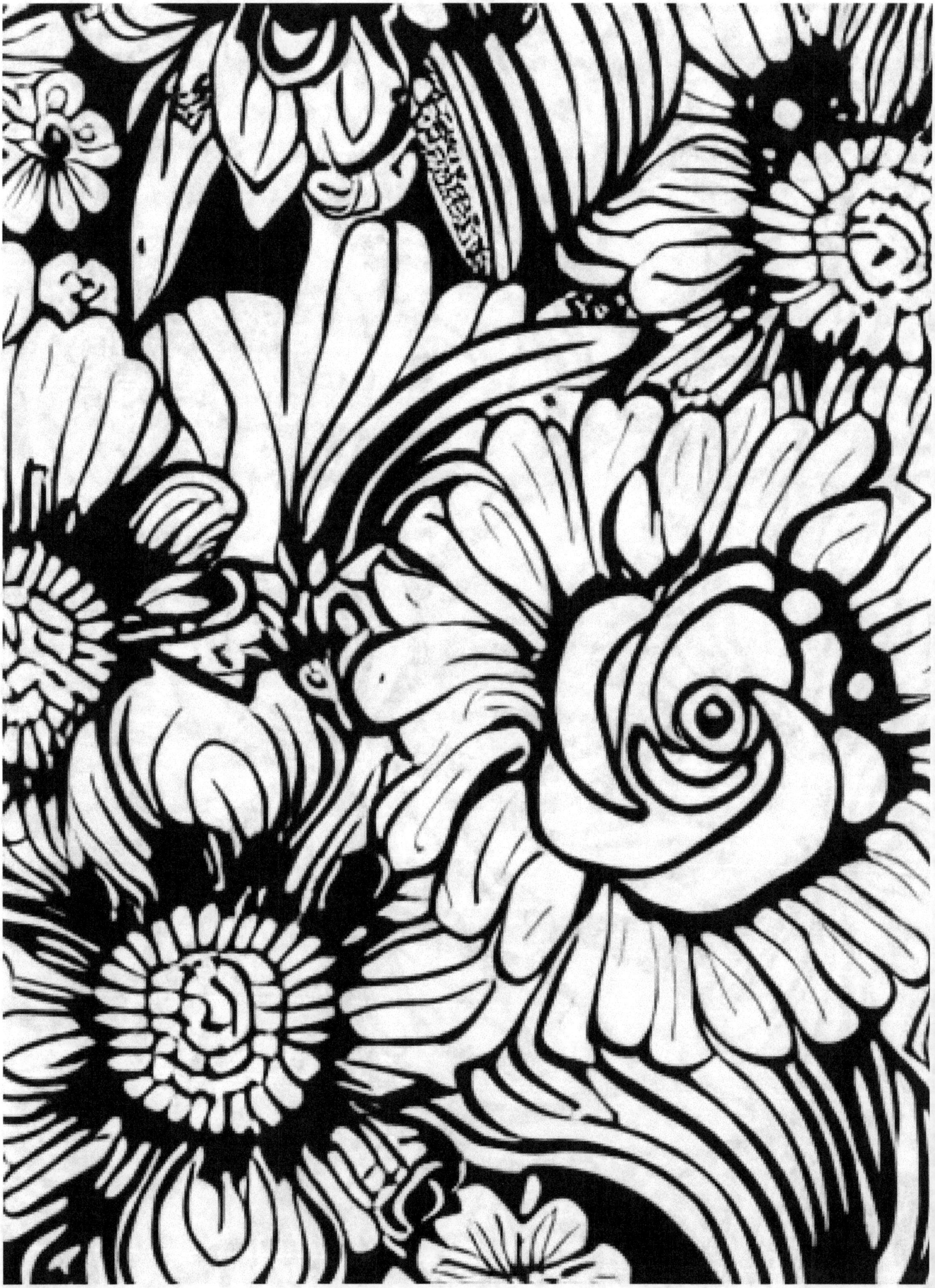

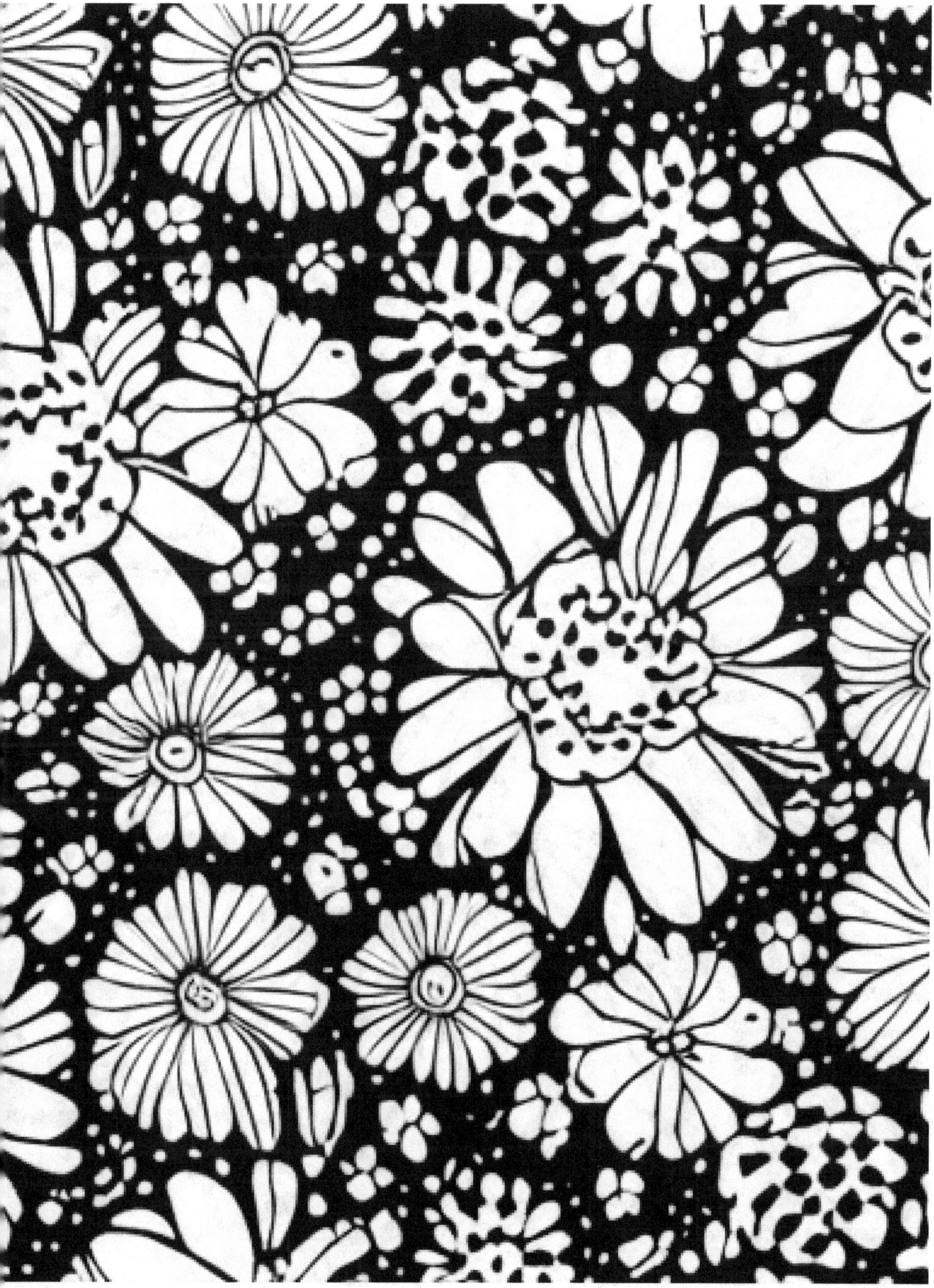

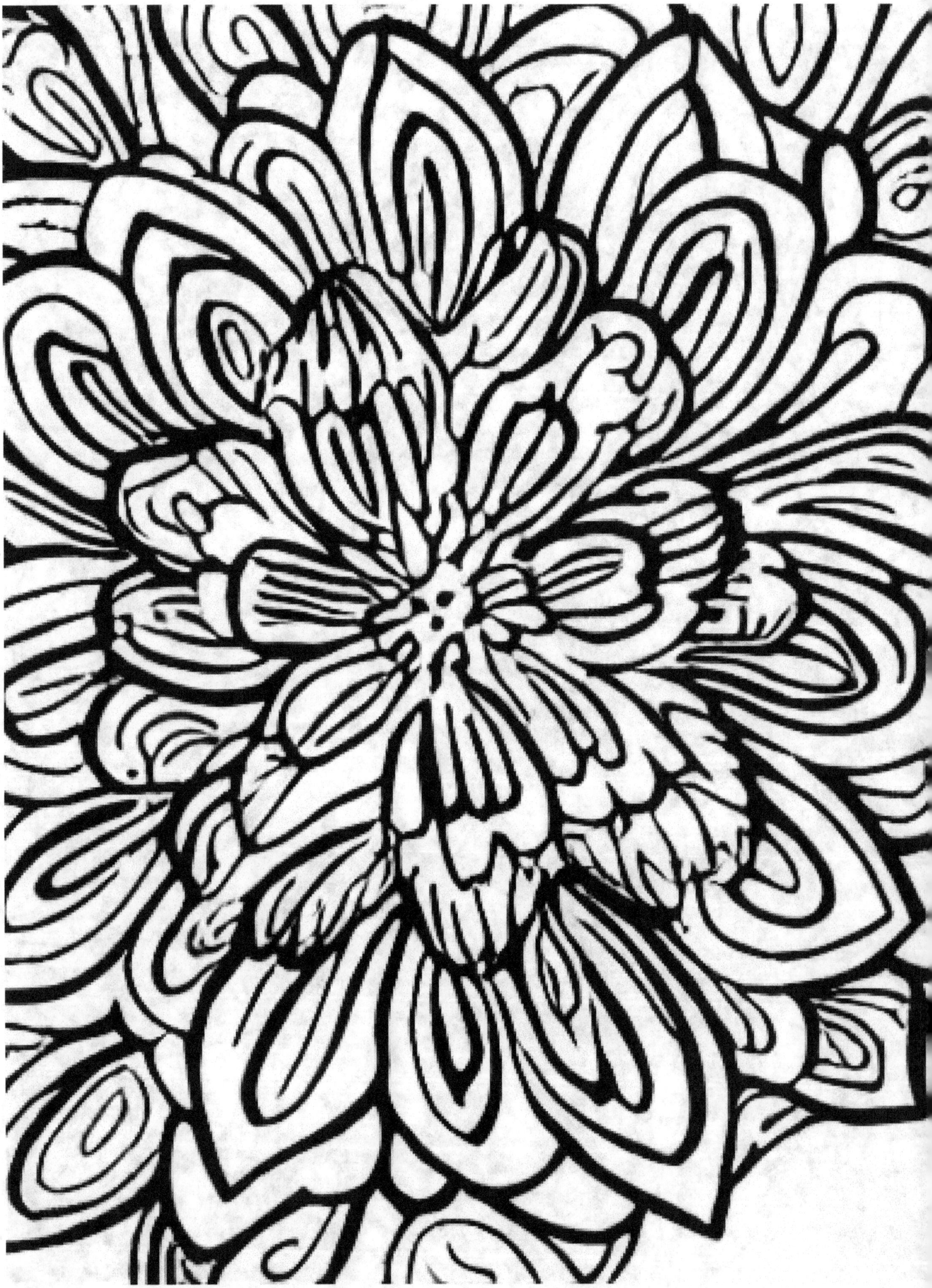

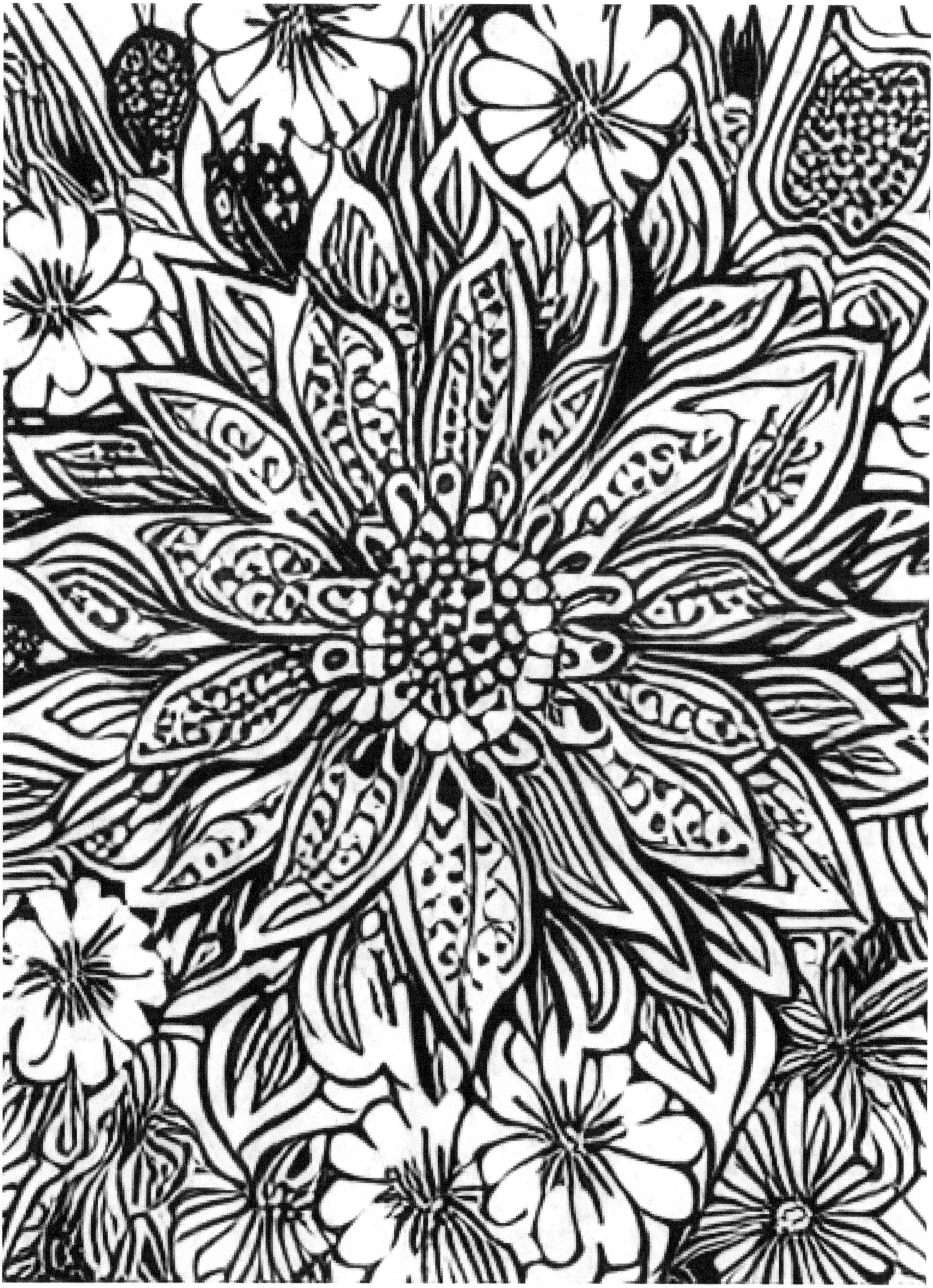

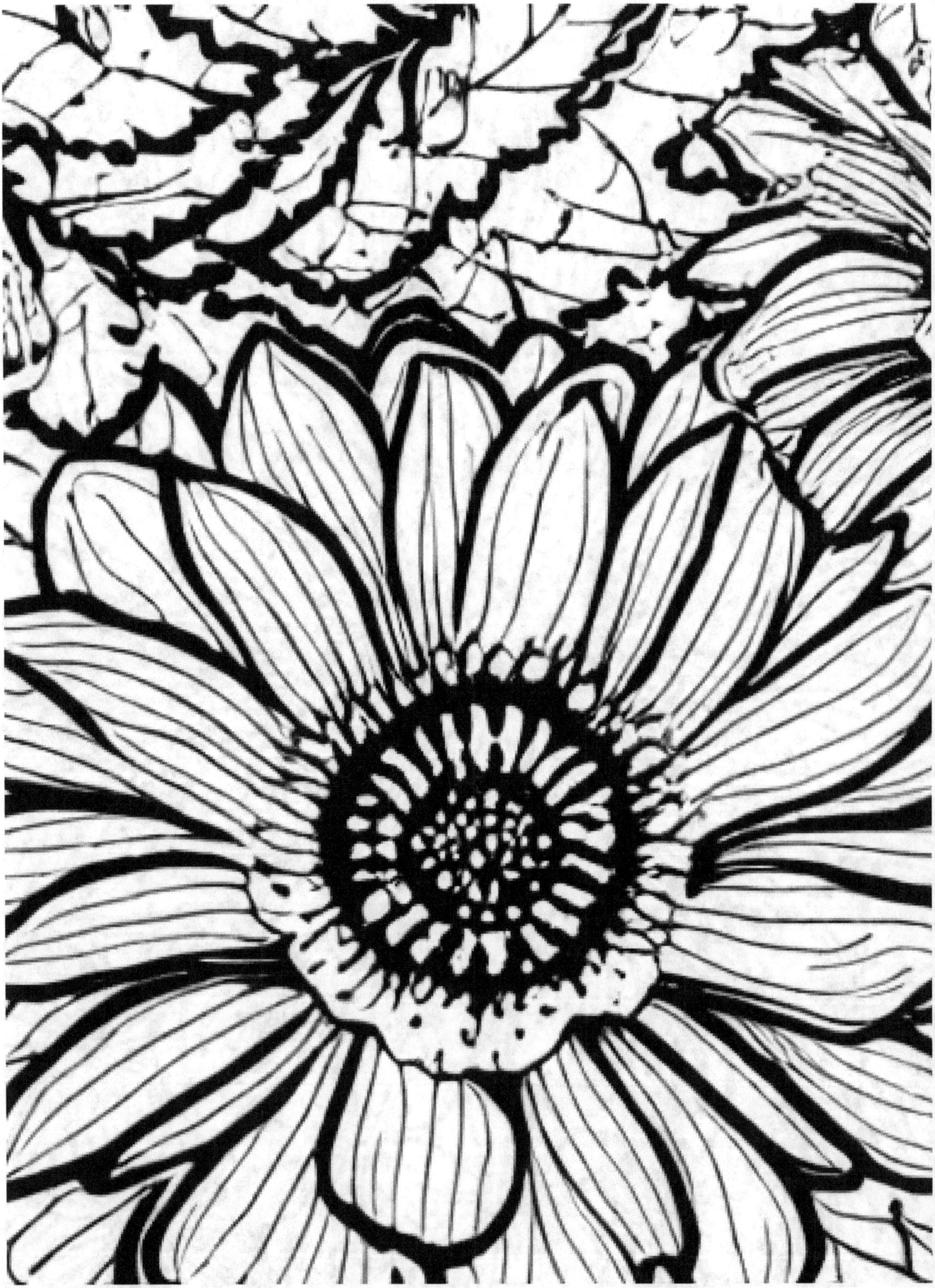

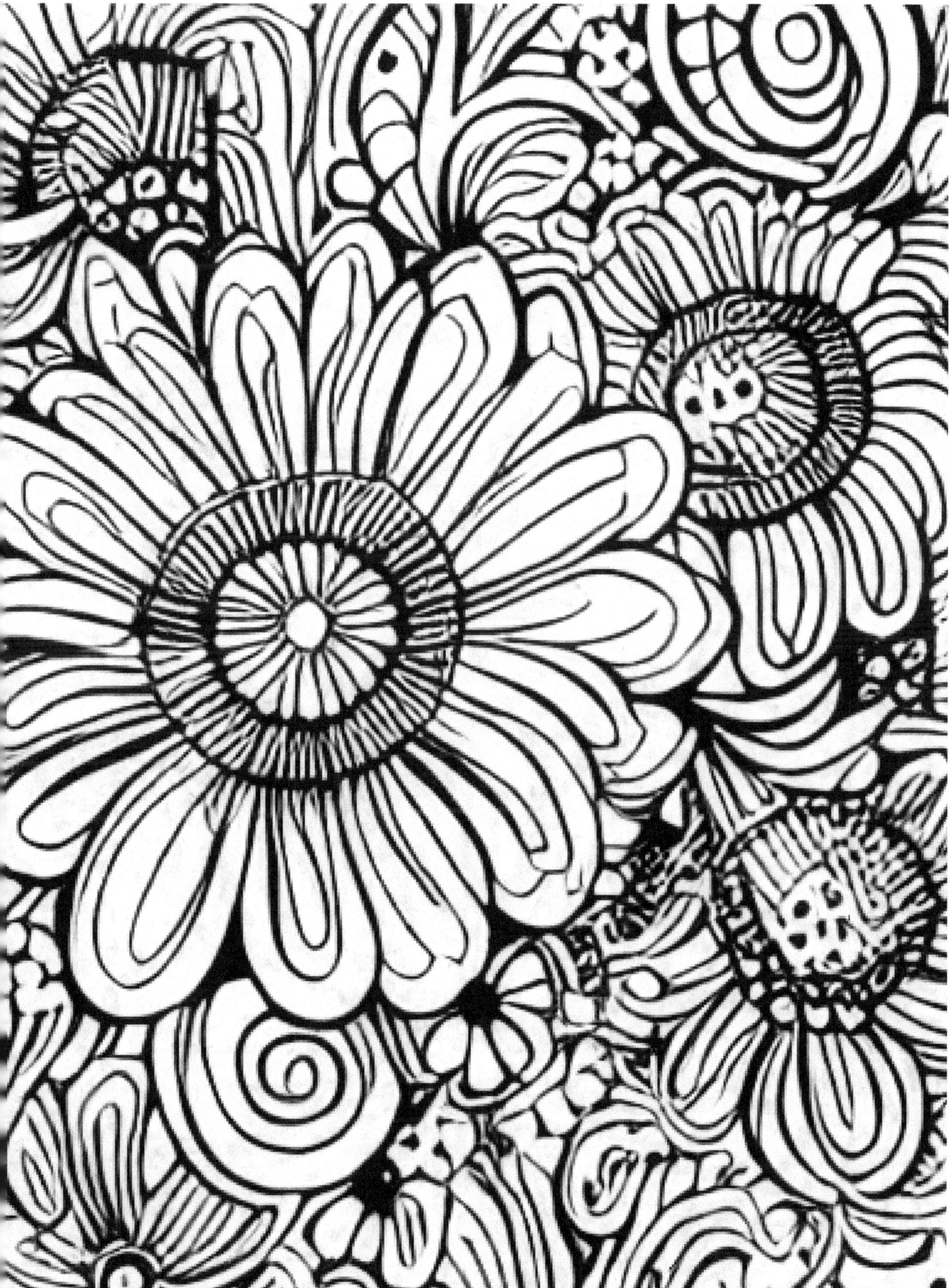

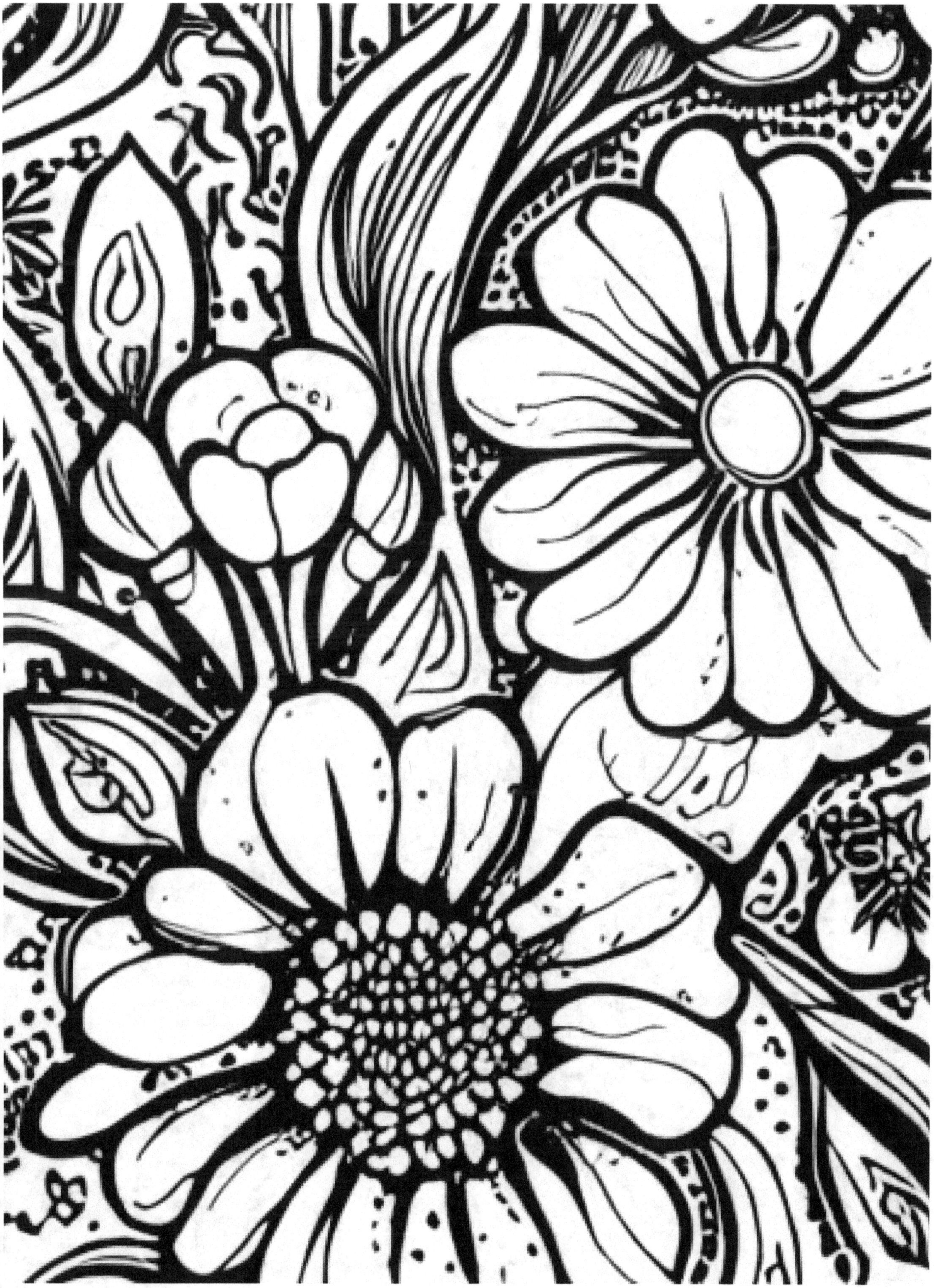

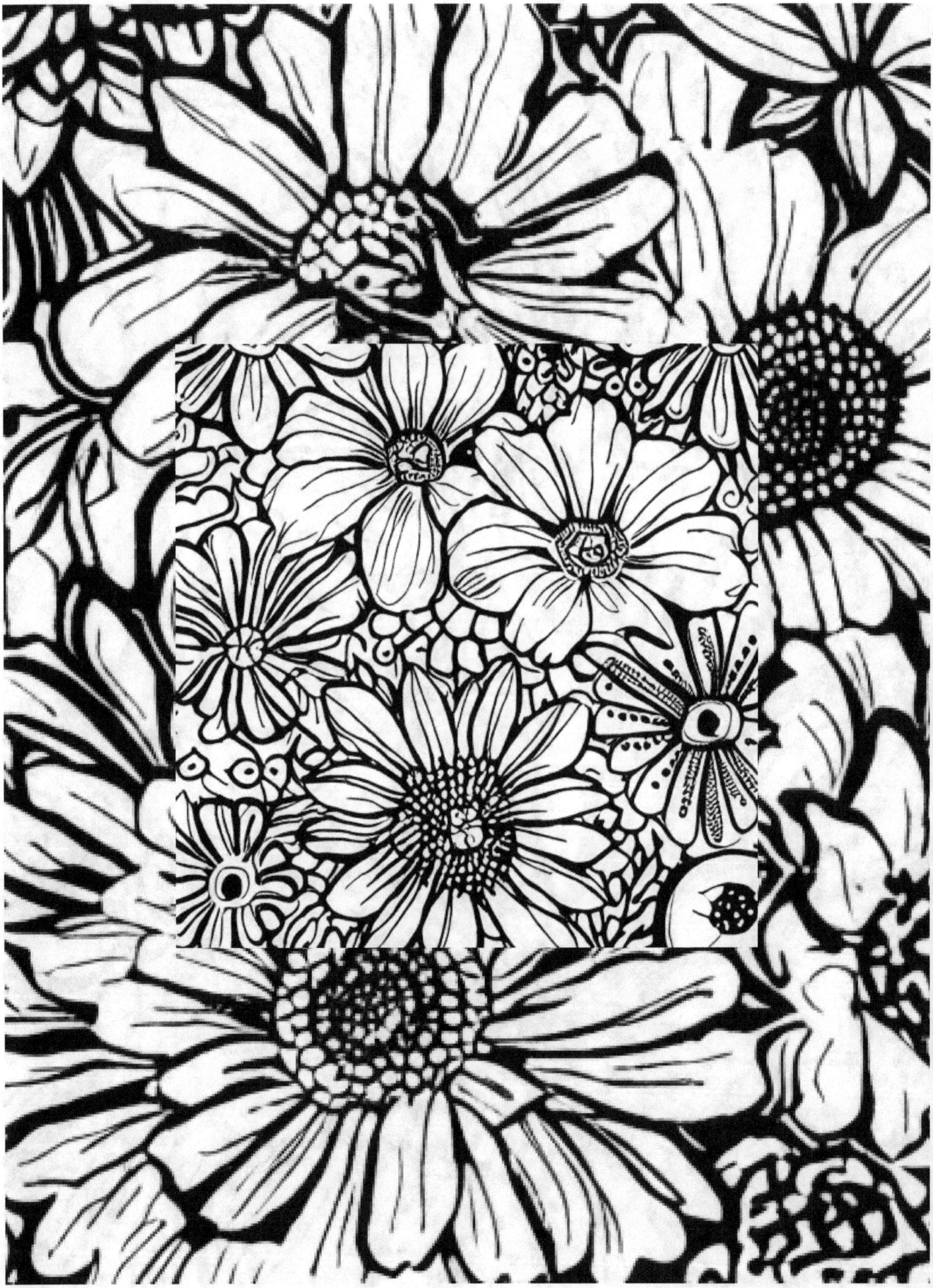

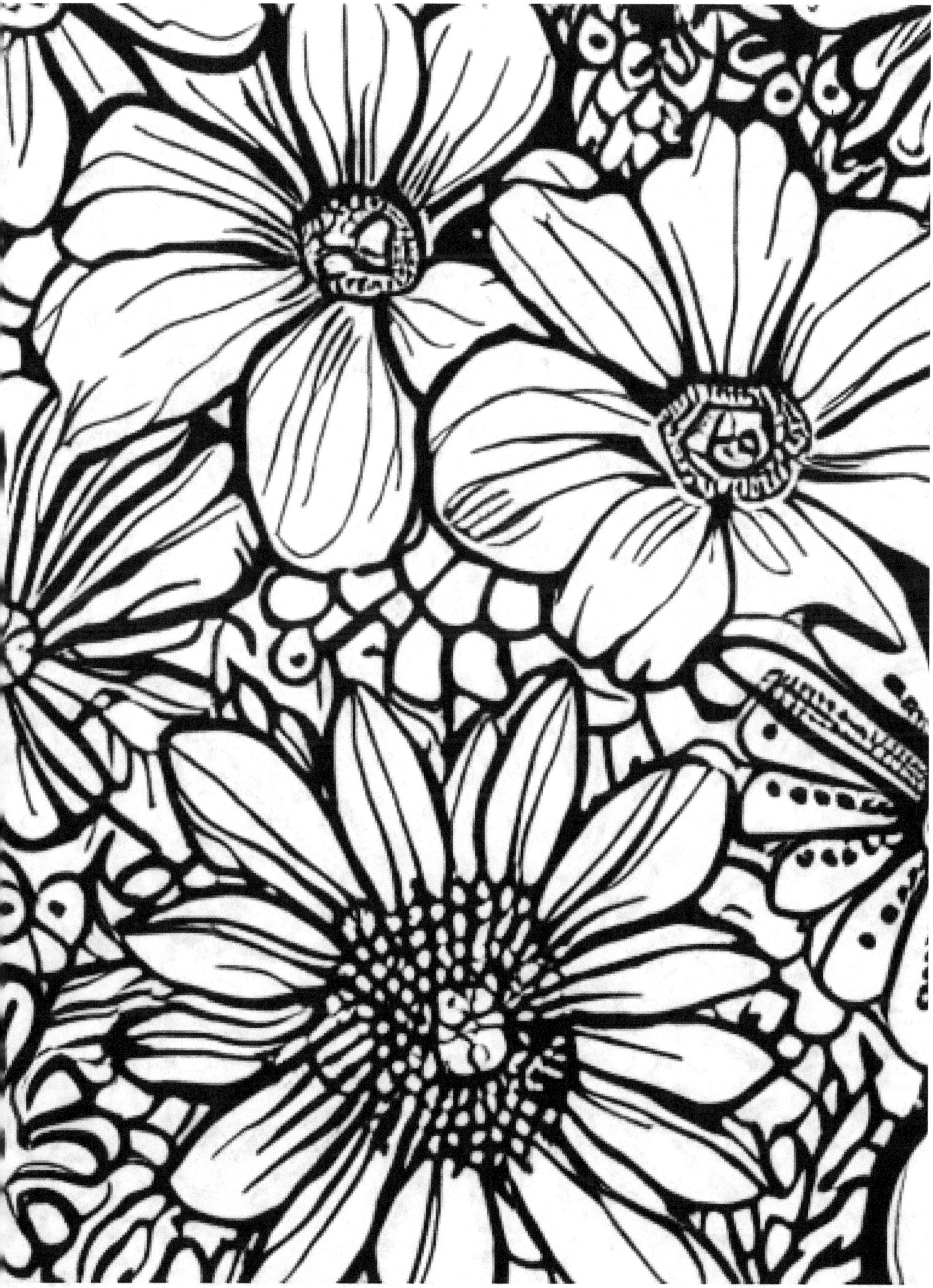

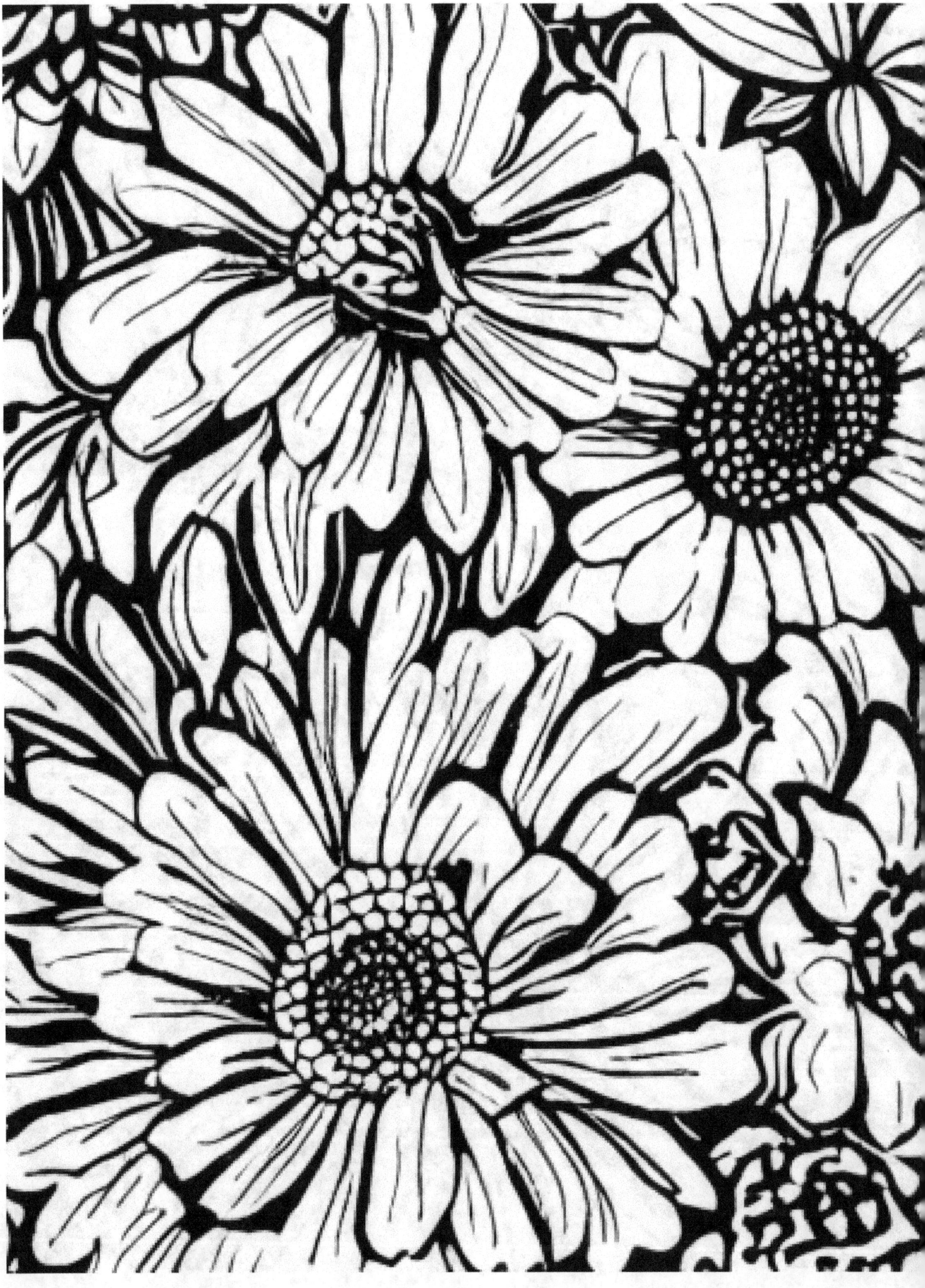

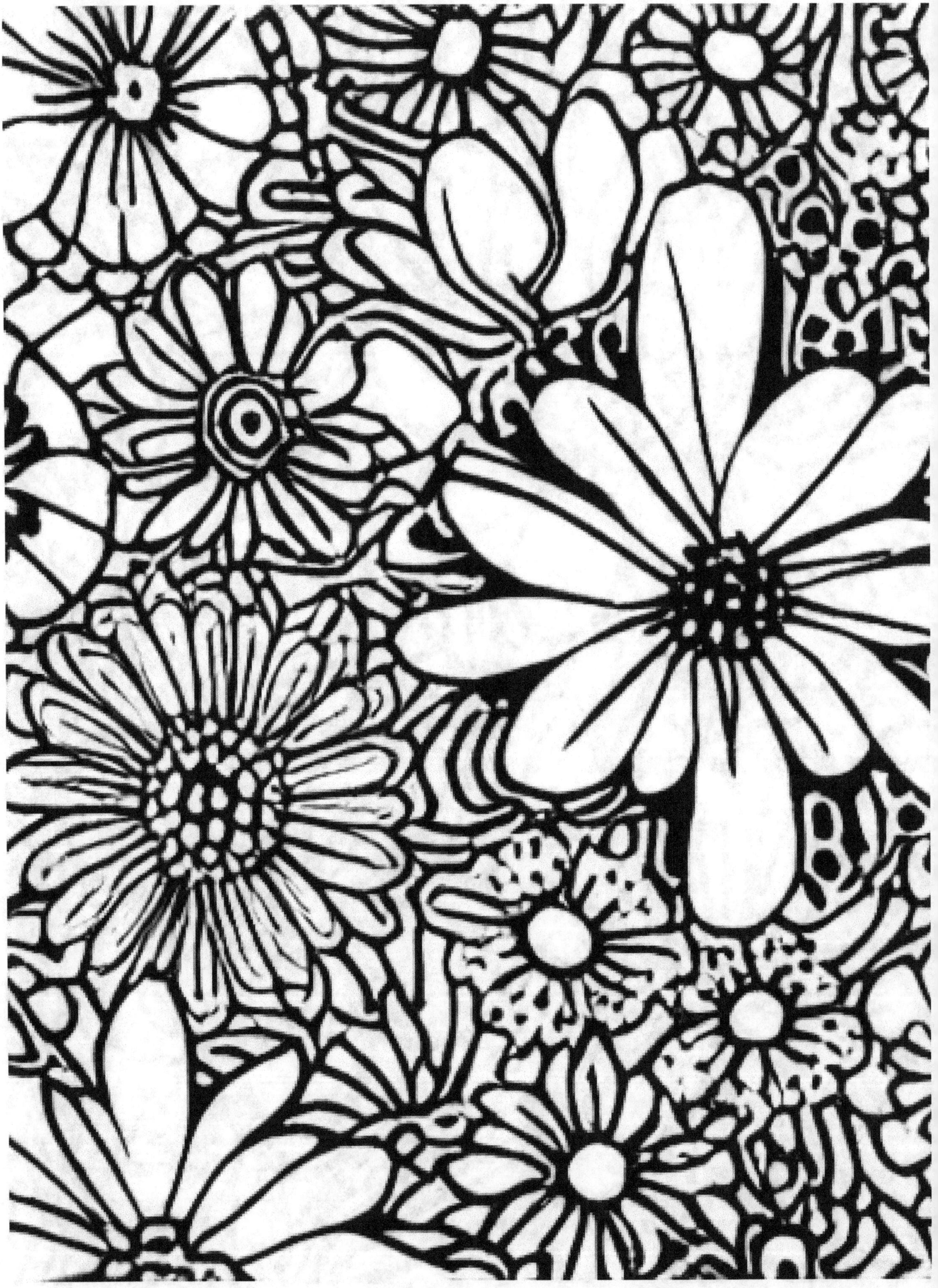

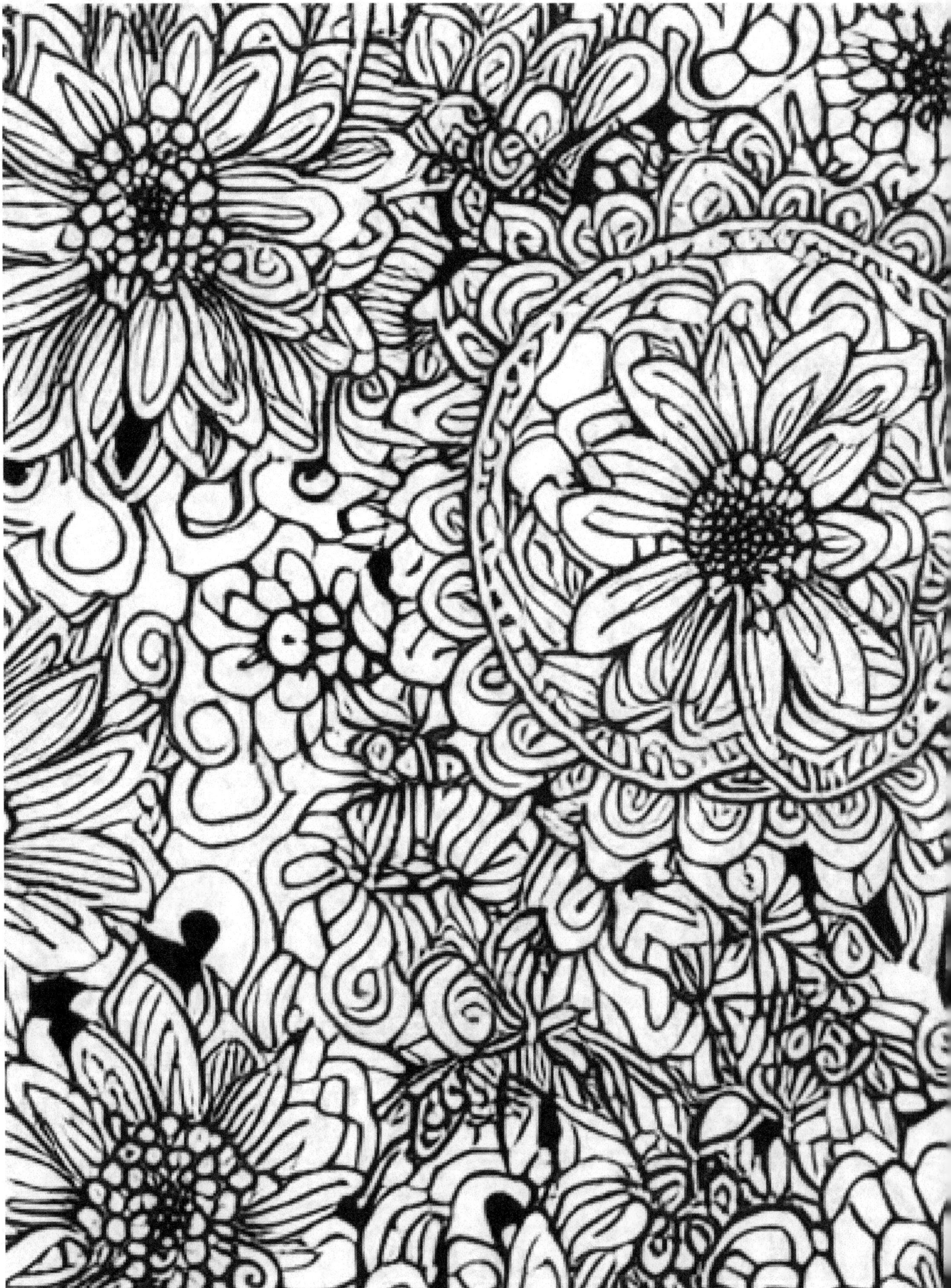

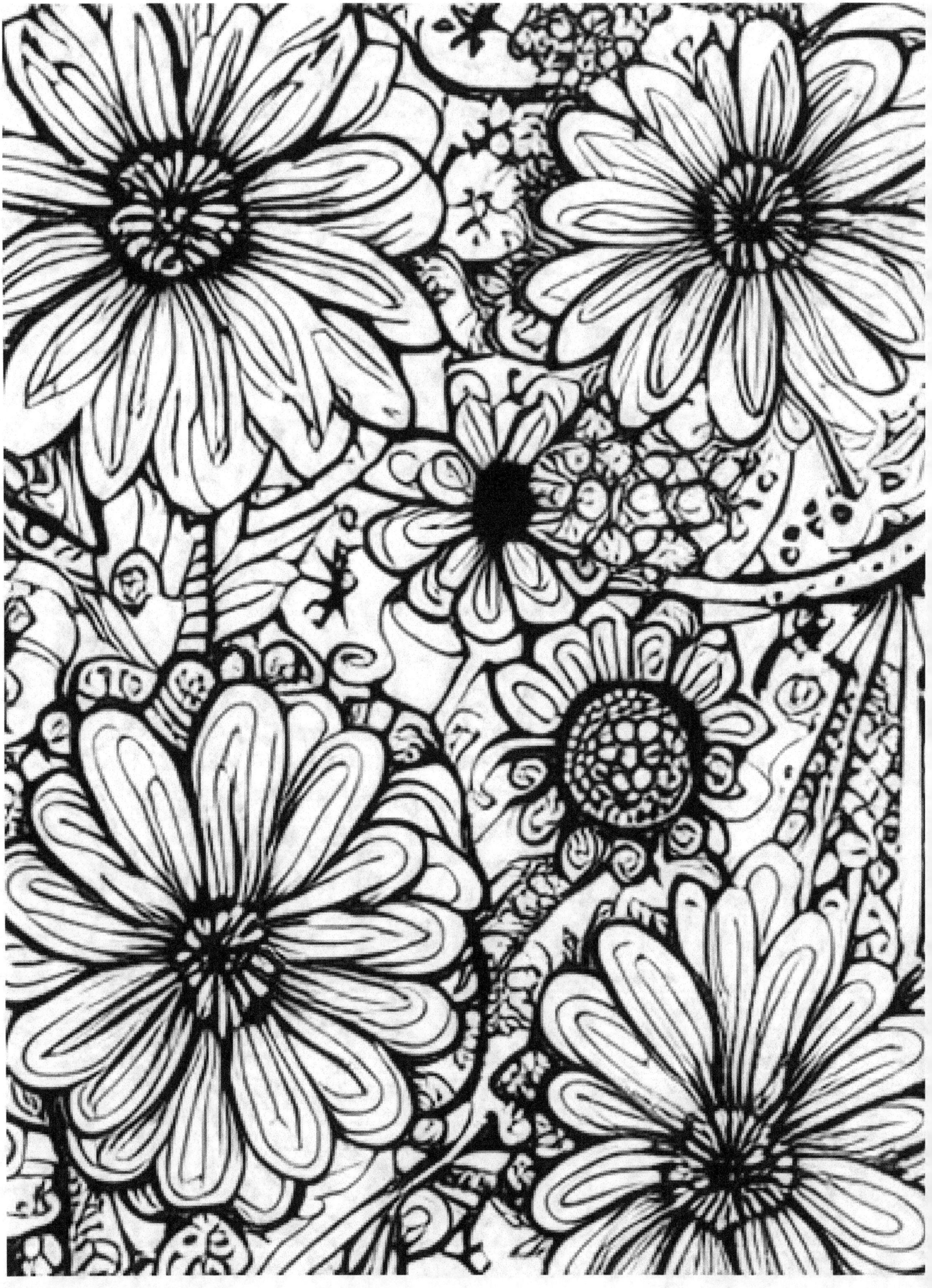

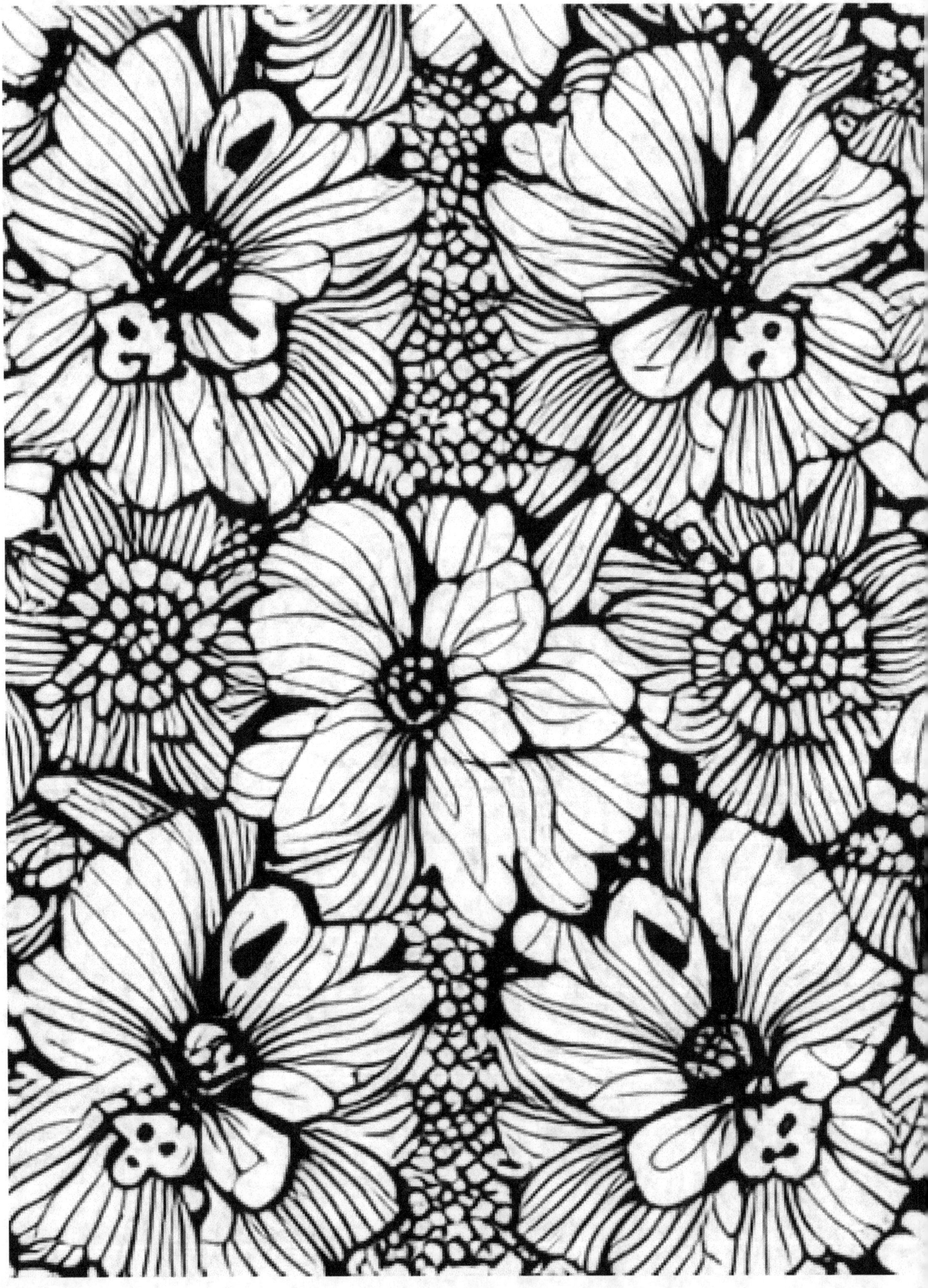

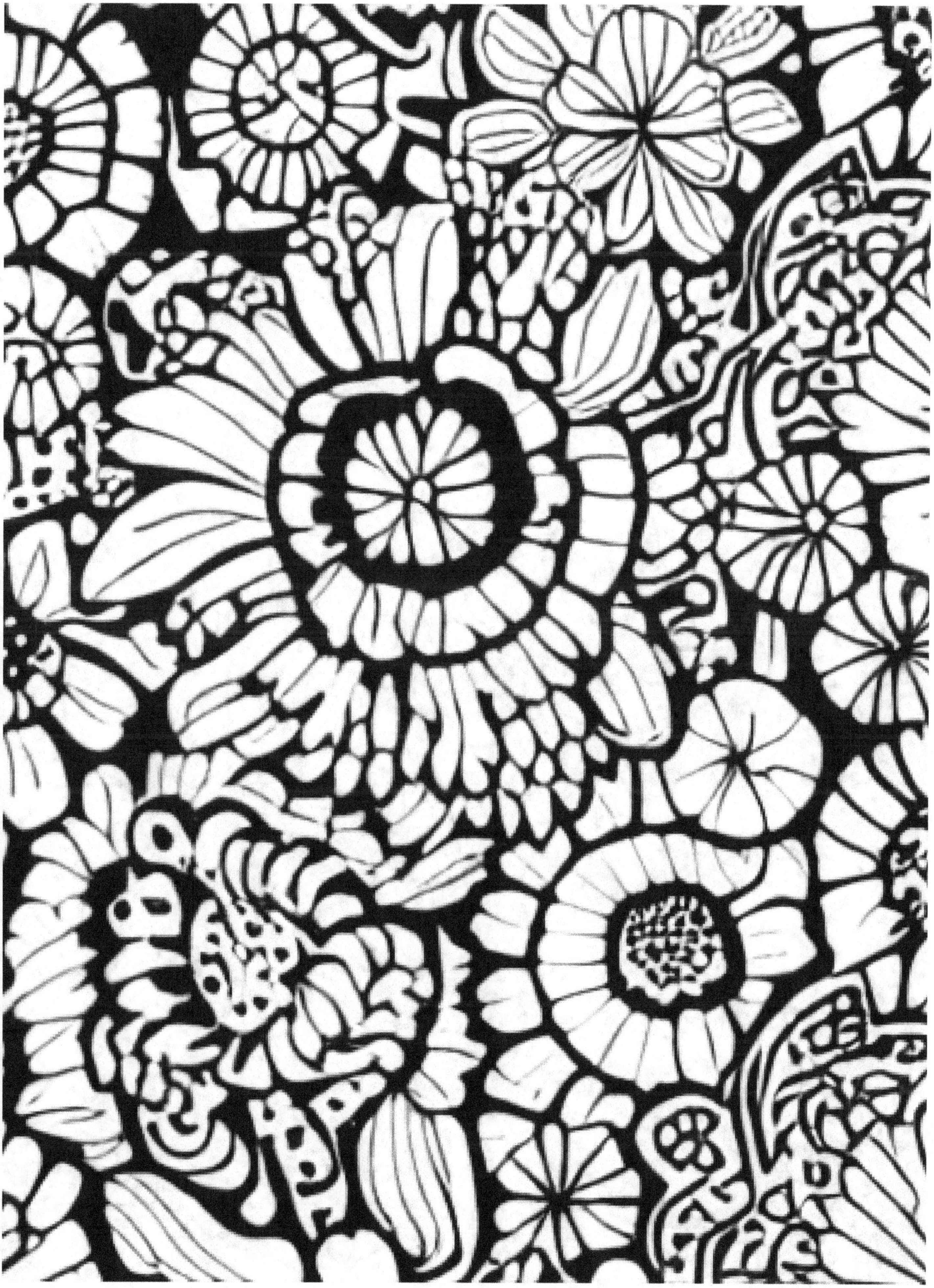

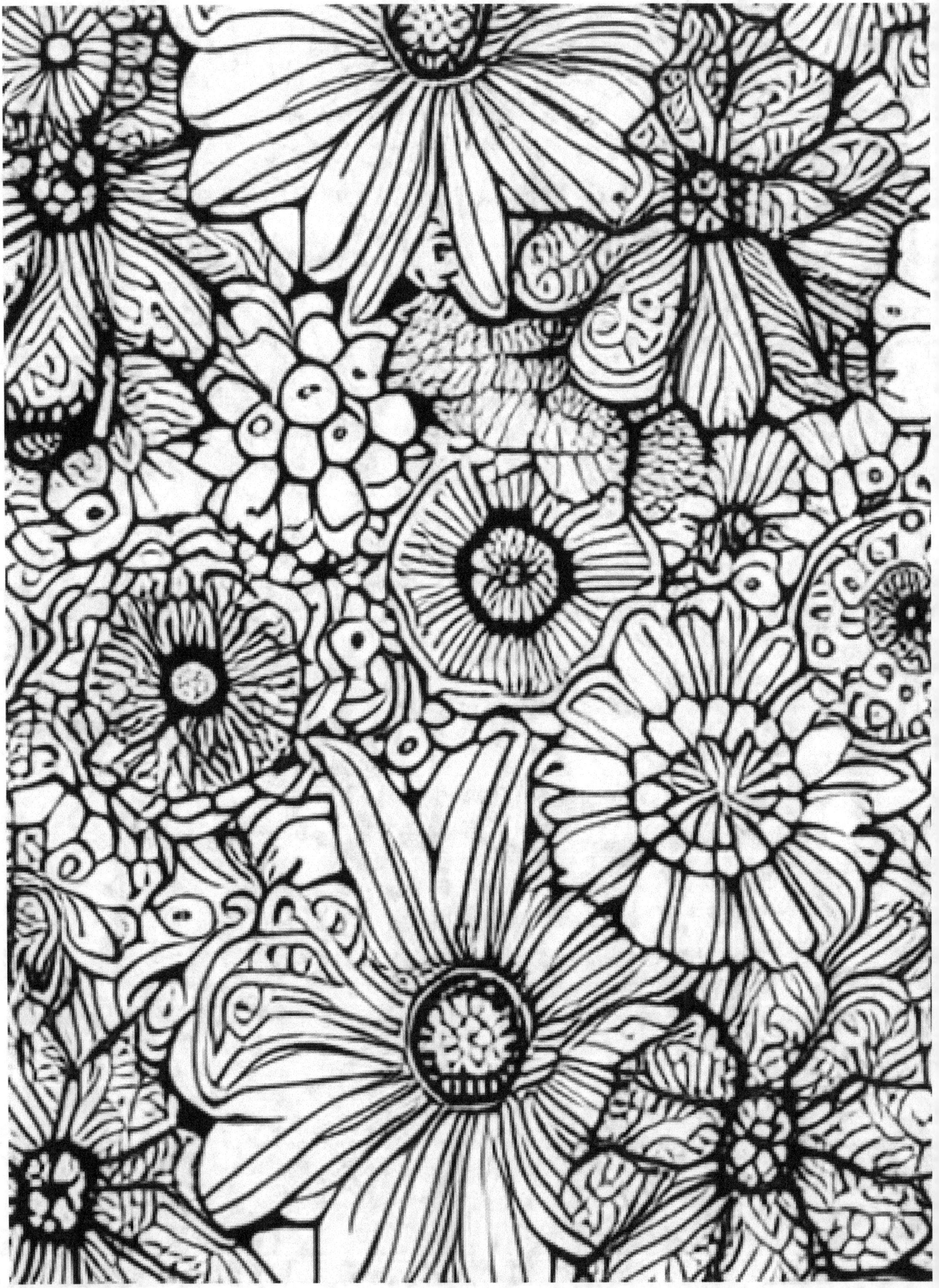

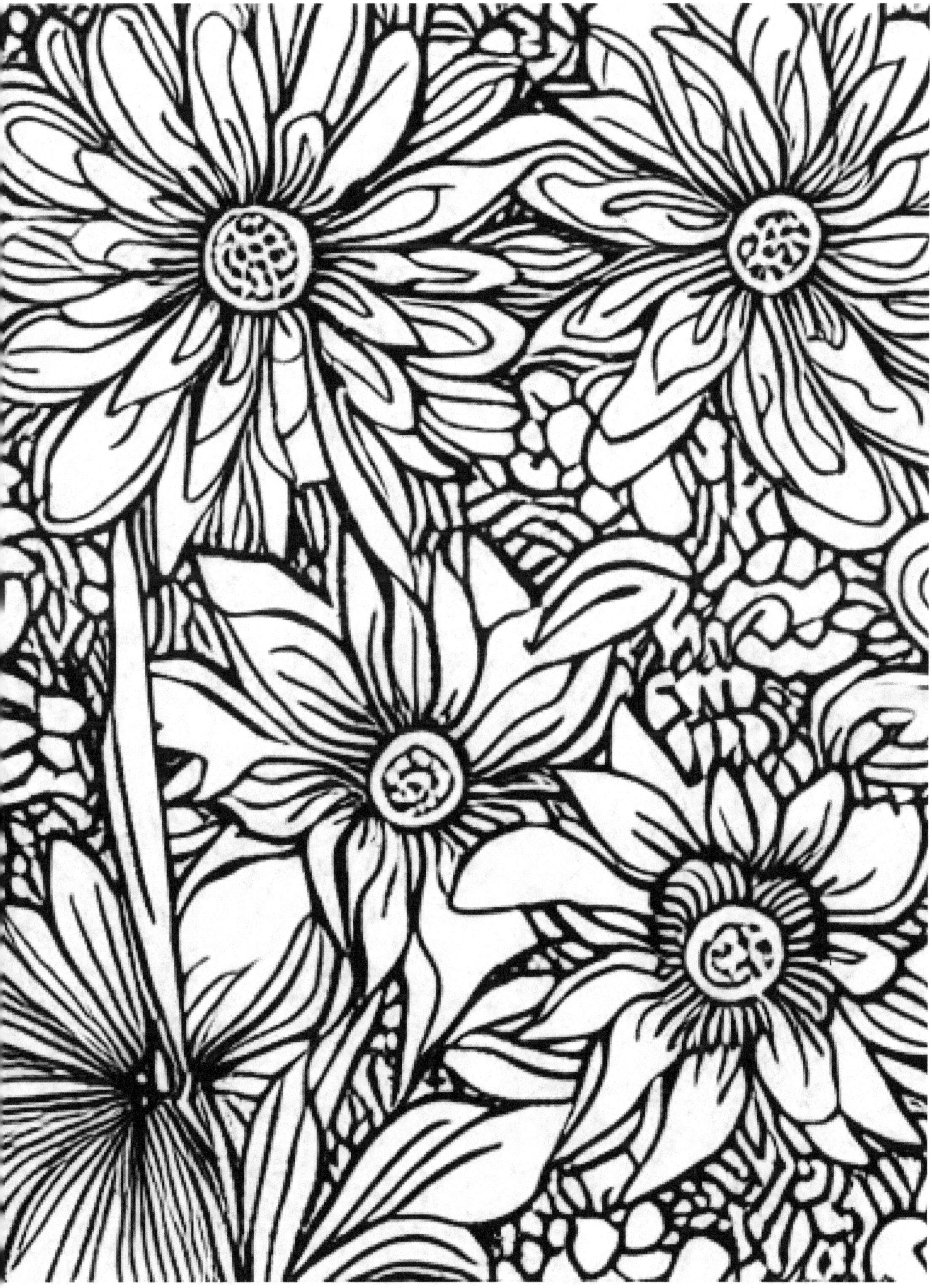

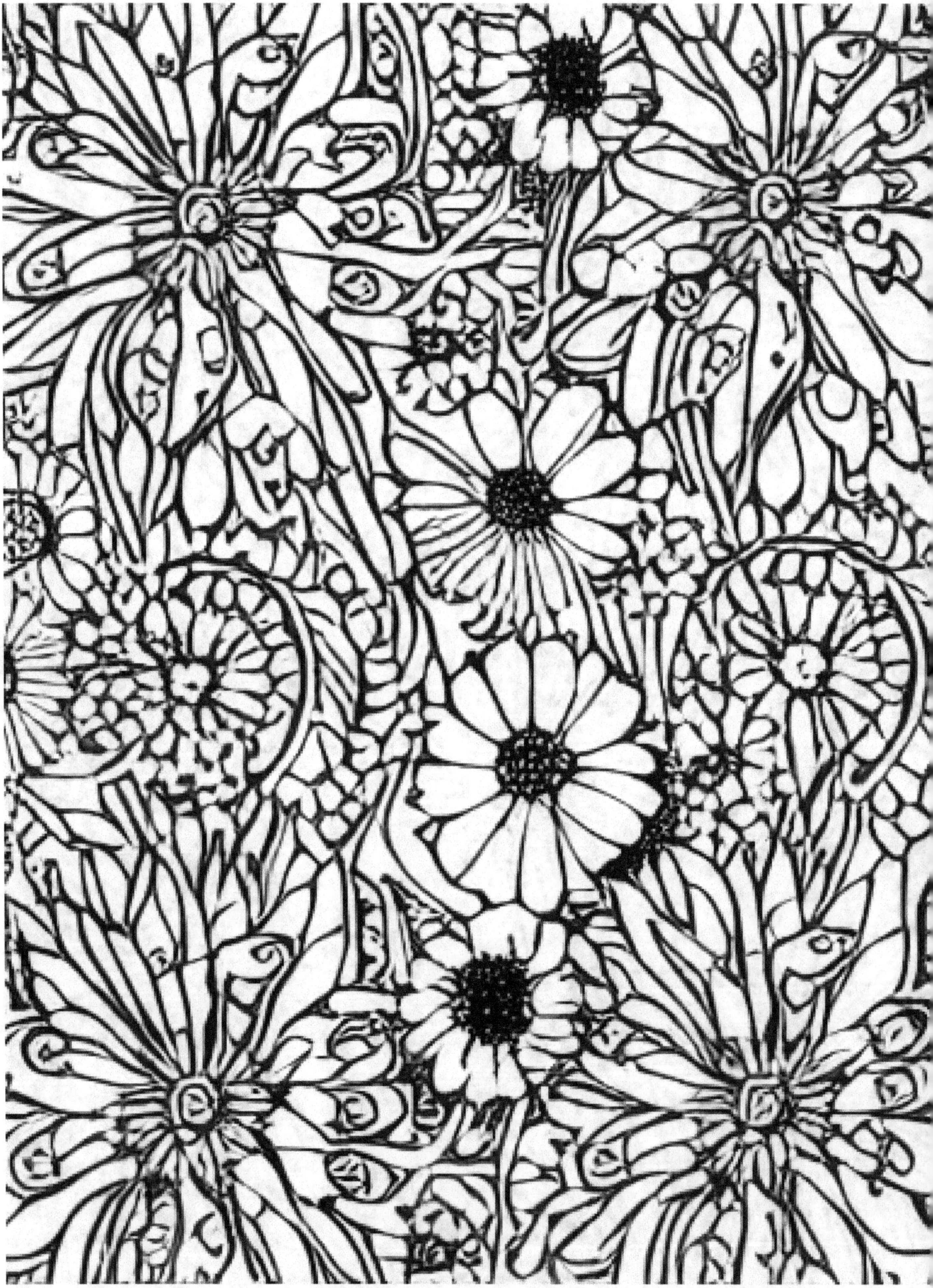

If you liked this coloring book, you would help me a lot by entering my profile and giving your opinion. Thank you so much!

JUANJO ALCANTARA

www.ingramcontent.com/pod-product-compliance
Lightning Source LLC
Chambersburg PA
CBHW081533220526
45467CB00010B/3166